Flower Gardening

BY THEODORE JAMES, JR.

GROSSET
GOOD LIFE
BOOKS

PUBLISHERS · GROSSET & DUNLAP · NEW YORK
A FILMWAYS COMPANY

Acknowledgments

Cover photograph by Mort Engel.

Except as noted below, all photographs by McDonald/Mulligan.

All-America Selections, p. 72; Bodger Seeds, Ltd. pp. 27, 31 (lower), 42; Burpee Seeds, pp. 7, 26, 31 (upper), 79 (upper); Jackson & Perkins, pp. 52, 54, 56, 58, 59; George W. Park Seed Co., Inc., p. 79 (lower).

Contents

1
Your Garden of Eden

It all began many years ago in the Garden of Eden. Adam and Eve wandered amid the loveliness of a garden that included hundreds of different flowering plants. Later, the Hanging Gardens of Babylon were so awe inspiring that they are still regarded as one of the Seven Wonders of the Ancient World. Long before the Europeans took to the serious cultivation of flowers, the Aztecs in Mexico used aqueducts to irrigate their gardens; their flowers were arranged in a scientific manner. And in the Far East, the Chinese were crossbreeding and hybridizing various species over two thousand years ago.

Well now, with such a heritage behind you, why don't you try your hand at growing flowers? Not only is it a rewarding avocation, but it is also very healthy. And it will give you a chance to express yourself artistically. No two gardens are ever alike.

You will find that your garden will become a sort of private refuge, a place to get away from the cares of the day and to spend some time communing with nature. Imagine the satisfaction you will receive when that "impossible" delphinium suddenly, from your care and nurturing, grows to its full seven feet and throws bloom that staggers not only you but everyone you know as well.

There is no doubt that a flower garden, healthy and in full bloom, is one of the most gratifying of all endeavors. If you make the effort to plant bulbs in the fall, you will receive a wonderful lift in the dreary days of late winter, when they courageously pop their heads up through the snow and bloom. "Ah, spring is on the way," you will say to yourself. The *Iris reticulata*, the snowflakes, the winter aconites, and the crocuses are blooming. Then, perhaps a few weeks later, the hyacinths and daffodils will flamboyantly display themselves against the just budding landscape. Then in May, when your flowering shrubs are in bloom and the trees are beginning to leaf out, a rainbow of tulips will be in bloom. It takes such little time, energy, and money to enjoy these miracles of nature.

As the season moves along, your spring-blooming perennials will treat you to their display. What could be more beautiful than an iris garden, with its majestic five-foot-high blooms, in full array? Then, your peonies, with their immense pink, white, red, and yellow blooms, will unfold. The biennials you planted the year before should now be ready to put on their show. The sweet

Early iris, late tulips, columbine, sweet violets, and leopards bane bloom in this spring garden.

williams, canterbury bells, wallflowers, digitalis, and forget-me-nots will be in bloom.

As June arrives, the rose garden takes on a particularly lovely appearance as all of those fall selections suddenly appear. The day lilies you selected will begin their show, as well as the trumpet and chalice lilies. The sequence is breathtaking. One type of flower after another buds, blooms, and withers.

In midsummer, the annuals you planted in the spring will be ready to fill in the voids left by the bulbs and perennials that have already bloomed. Then in the fall, the annuals will be in full stride, and your chrysanthemums will present that final blaze of devastating color before winter sets in. It is nature's show, but you've been the one who has made it happen!

This book is meant primarily to encourage you to plant flowers. Anybody can grow a successful flower garden with just a little effort and money. You can confine yourself to a small patch, or if you are more ambitious and have plenty of land to cultivate, perhaps you could plan a garden border over one hundred feet long. But regardless of the scale you tackle, do plant flowers.

The growth of all flowers is explained in the following chapters. You will learn how to grow annuals, which complete the total growth cycle in one year; the perennials, which continue to grow year after year; the biennials, which take two years to complete their growth cycle; roses; the hardy bulbs, which can remain in the ground year in and year out; and the tender bulbs, which must be lifted out every fall to protect them from winter's cold. There are also chapters on climbing plants, on building a beautiful rock garden, and on pests and diseases.

Study this book and visit your local nurseries, arboretums, public gardens, and county garden centers to familiarize yourself with the various species of flowers. Ask your friends, neighbors, and relatives about their gardens and what plants they find are particularly satisfactory in your area. You will find, once you have become interested in gardening, that an entire new dimension will be added to your life. Even if you know next to nothing about gardening, there are many plants that simply will not fail. You have nothing to lose but a little time, energy, and money and you have all the glory of beautiful flowers to gain.

You've seen advertisements in the newspapers and magazines that read something like: "Imagine, you too can grow flowers like these!" Well you can! So get yourself a trowel and some seeds, bulbs, or plants, and get to work. Or rather, get to the pleasure of flower gardening. You won't regret it.

Opposite: *One of the nicest places to establish a flower garden is near the entry of your home. Here hybrid petunias, annuals, bloom in the foreground with floribunda roses giving fragrant flowers beyond.*

Another favorite place to plant a flower garden is around your outdoor living area.

2
Planning Your Flower Garden

Almost anyone can plan a flower garden properly if he takes the time. Indeed, there are always problems, but very few are so insurmountable that the average gardener cannot solve them. Most successful flower gardens are planned and planted over a period of years. Therefore, it is imperative that before you do anything, you sit down and plan. By reaching for the pencil, not for the spade, you will save yourself a good deal of transplanting and rearranging.

Purchase some graph paper, get a ruler, and set about your plan. First measure the size of your property and draw lines indicating this on the graph paper. Use one square per foot of space. Next draw your house on the plan. Include the house, the doors, windows, garage doors, driveway, and existing trees or shrubs, and anything else that is on your property. Again, use one square per foot. Now you have before you the basic scheme with which you will work.

Next decide where you want to place your flower garden. There are many things to consider when you decide this. Keep in mind full sun, shade, partial shade, high spots, low spots, drainage, views from your windows, house access, etc. Then and only then, lay out your permanent flower beds on your basic scheme.

Laying Out the Bed

Plan to mark off and outline your flower bed at least one or two weeks before you begin planting. Set stakes at either end of the straight lines and tie stout string, rope, or clothesline tightly between the stakes. For curved edging, use a garden hose. A rubber hose will stay put, but a plastic hose should be filled with water and capped at both ends in order to stay in place. You can buy these caps at a hardware store or nursery. Sprinkle the hose with lime so that it stands out visibly in the grass. When you lift the hose, the white lime outline of the curved edge will remain. For straight edges, use a square-cut spade to cut the sod; and for curved edges, use an edger, a special tool designed for this kind of work.

Now you will want to dig a trench two feet deep. Once you have done this, prepare the soil thoroughly. That is, enrich it with recommended fertilizer, compost, peat moss, and other organic matter. Test the acidity or alkalinity of the soil and adjust it properly with copper sulfate or lime. You can do this by purchasing a simple soil-testing kit at your local nursery. Your local pharmacist can also test your soil for you. Once you have done this, let the soil settle thoroughly for a week or more before starting your planting.

Paper Planting

Now take a separate piece of graph paper and a pencil and make a scale drawing of your flower border or bed. A good ratio is one foot to a half inch on the paper. This is the time to experiment. Get some tracing paper and lay it over the drawing of your flower bed. Try many versions, since it is easier to do this on paper than to move plants around later.

Select eight or more basic perennials and bulbs as the backbone of your permanent bed. In selecting perennials, strive to include flowers that bloom for a long period and foliage that remains orderly and attractive for most of the season. Also, be sure that you consider the succession of bloom; that is, plan for early, midseason, and late-season blooming displays. Look at illustrations in newspapers, magazines, or garden books for ideas. Work only one section or part of the border at a time.

Draw in two or three groupings of the taller perennials for the back of the border, two or three groupings of medium-sized perennials for the middle, and one or two groupings for the front and side. Each of the groupings you select should be similar in shape to the border to achieve the best design. Plan to have groups of tall plants come forward in some places. This avoids a stilted look.

Then sketch in permanent edging plants for the front of your garden. There are two different ways you can plan this. Either use all of one kind of flower, preferably an evergreen which will be attractive in the winter, or two or more kinds of edging plants of which at least one should be evergreen.

Then back up the edging plants with filler flowers to bridge the gaps between your major displays. Plant them in groups of three, five, or seven of one kind. They should be less dominant in appearance, should bloom only a short time, or should have foliage that disappears or fails to hold and turns rather ragged. Columbine, bleeding heart, and Oriental poppy are three flowers of the filler type. These can be supplemented with annuals once they have turned shabby or have died back.

Repeat these drifts at intervals throughout the other sections of your border to give it unity and to tie it together. Always allow a greater distance between these groups themselves and the individual plants that comprise the group. Remember, the more space you can leave between the plant groups, the healthier your plants and thus your garden will be. If they look somewhat sparse the first year, remember they will fill in quickly in most cases. Annuals will take care of the bare spots during the first season.

On another piece of paper, or next to your garden sketch, list all of the plant types you plan to use. Write down the eventual height, spread, time of bloom, length of bloom, and color with corresponding numbers on your sketch. This will help you recheck your plant selection. Check that you have allowed sufficient space, have good height relationship, and have selected the colors you want. Also check to be sure you will have continuous bloom in your garden. Jot down exactly when you are supposed to sow the seeds of the annuals you have selected to fill in.

This exercise will assist you in keeping records for your orders and also, should your labels get lost, you can locate spring bulbs and other plants whose tops die down during the summer.

Balance

If you wish to create a formal garden, balance is the key factor. Repeat the same plants on both sides of the center. If informality is your end, place one or several tall plants on one side of the center and a mass of low-growing plants on the other side. Always keep in mind that the solid forms have a greater impact on the eye than the more delicate open plants. Texture, as such, is more visually powerful than smooth surfaces. Striking colors are more vivid than pastels. If you are planning a small garden, a formal arrangement is more satisfactory simply because it is more obvious and more placid than an asymmetrical one.

Unifying Your Garden with the Landscape

Borders are always more satisfactory if they blend with the landscape. If your landscape contains trees, shrubs, and vines, select plants that complement their bloom. For instance, white flowering plants combine effectively with white spirea or white dogwood. Climbing roses, which bloom in early June, blend well with peonies and the spectacular tall bearded iris.

Repeating Plant Groups and Colors

For unity, repeat your plant groupings and colors in sequence at various intervals. Compose the colors so that they appear throughout the border. Do not plant your garden so that there is a solid block of color on one side and a green oasis on the other.

Geraniums bloom in this garden from spring 'til frost.

Varieties in Planting

Avoid busyness, spottiness, or confusion. Try to attain a consistent, pleasant transition among the varieties selected. Keep in mind that smaller, more delicate plants and medium-sized plants are more in scale with a smaller border.

Foliage should be kept in mind, since its form, texture, and size can add a great deal to the interest of the border. Coarse leaves of plants, such as hollyhock and hosta, contrast nicely with the finer texture of columbine leaves. Medium-sized leaves combine well with linum's fine, narrow leaves.

Also keep in mind contrasting forms. Use a tall, spike-type plant here and there to contrast with bushier and flat-topped plants. The bushy plants present fine masses of color, while the columnar plants add accents, grace, and charm.

Keep in Mind the Background

Always remember that a neutral background or partial enclosure enhances the beauty of a flower garden. Objectional views are shut out, and the eye is permitted to concentrate on the flower garden. Trees and shrubs, hedges, walls, or fences (properly planted with vines or partially hidden by the flowers themselves) add to the beauty of your garden.

If you use hedges, allow them to grow naturally, since they look better and are less work than those formally clipped. A split rail fence of cedar, locust, or redwood eventually weathers nicely and naturally complements your scheme. In addition, this type of fence offers no root competition to your flowers. In edging your garden, bricks laid so that the brick length supplies the width of the strip are always effective. If you place the bricks level with and at the edge of the flower border, they allow space for one wheel of the lawn mower, simplifying the chore of grass cutting and minimizing hand trimming. In addition, the border shape is retained and the garden is separated from the grass so that encroaching plants cannot grow into your lawn. These strips are decorative and permanent, and they provide a neat, orderly appearance.

Plant Heights and Shapes

As a rule, use low-spreading plants for edging, well-rounded medium plants for filling, and tall spiky plants for backing. This helps achieve a good design in your flower bed. Select several very dominant plants (such as lilies, delphiniums, gas plants, or irises) and repeat them at intervals throughout the border. These few accents in crucial spots can alleviate a monotonous look, making your garden distinct and interesting. With the spires of hardy lilies, delphiniums, and the like rising above the lower, rounded masses of phlox and other perennials, the eye is given a lift.

Between the accents, mass flowers by grouping together several plants of one kind. You will achieve a more effective look if you plant in drifts. Try to avoid planting in a regular shape or position. Stagger your planting so that one plant is not directly in front or in back of another plant.

Selecting Colors

You can achieve your own personal effect with color. Some people like strong colors and striking combinations, such as scarlet Oriental poppies with blue delphiniums or vibrant yellow flowers next to strong purples. Since direct sunlight lightens colors, you can do this freely if you choose.

Another possibility is to blend related colors; for example, you could use yellows and yellow oranges. For small gardens, you might consider using all one color. An all-white garden, for example, can be breathtaking, particularly in the evening. Many white flowers bloom at night and are heavily fragrant. If you do decide on a one-color garden, vary the hues; that is, if you select red, include the palest pinks and the most vibrant maroons to give your garden some contrast.

There are a few rules of thumb to consider in selecting color. Warm colors make objects appear nearer to the eye; cool colors make them appear further away. In wooded areas there is no sunlight to neutralize colors; hence, vivid

Dutch iris, daffodils and baby's breath are wonderful flowers to grow for making bouquets to enjoy indoors.

Enriched soil, plenty of water and lots of sunlight will produce a border like this one, literally a breathtaking display of bloom. The flowers include petunias, Shasta daisies, delphiniums and hollyhocks.

colors may appear garish. Pastels and white flowers look best in the shade. Warm colors are conspicuous, sensuous, and aggressive to the eye. Cool colors are calm and restful.

How Many Plants Should You Get for Your Garden?

As a rule of thumb, three plants are needed for each drift of flowers in order to make a reasonable showing. It is always difficult to generalize about flower gardens, since there are many factors to consider. Nonetheless a few generalizations follow.

Tall Plants: Many tall plants are invasive and need space. For instance, a good-sized phlox plant should have about four square feet and a large peony about six square feet. Give tall plants plenty of room to grow, since the more light and air they have, the shorter and stockier they will be. This may eliminate the necessity of staking them during the summer. Many tall perennials also have large root systems and need plenty of room for root space.

For most large plants, allow one square yard of planting space.

If you are trying to economize, keep in mind that most perennials multiply rapidly. If you purchase only one or two plants the first year, by the second or third year you can divide them and have many more.

Medium-sized Plants: Keep in mind the branching element when selecting medium-sized plants. Allow from one square foot for compact, upright plants to one square yard for free-branching plants. Medium-sized plants can be planted either in clumps (say three to a clump) or in drifts (which is often preferred, since when a species completes its bloom, its absence is less noticeable than if it were in an isolated clump).

Edging Plants: Allow from one to two square feet of space for each edging plant. Plants such as candytuft and dwarf lavender, along with many other highly suitable edging plants, may sprawl as they age; however, they rarely run rampant. If you want fast results, plant the fast spreaders and place them one foot apart.

Purchasing Your Plants

Be sure you place your order early so that you will have a good selection of varieties available for spring or fall planting. Keep in mind that each dollar you spend will entail hours of work and perhaps even years of waiting. Start with something good.

If you do have to cut corners financially, steer clear of the newer varieties. They are usually offered to specialists and collectors, and they are high in price because they are scarce. Buy the tried and true, which are usually as good as the new and novel. King Alfred Daffodil, for example, is one of the oldest and yet still one of the finest varieties of narcissus offered. As new varieties are proven superior to the older ones, they will be produced in greater quantity, and the prices will eventually drop.

Another way to economize is to buy small plants of high quality and let them grow to specimen size in your own garden. Or you can propagate your own plants.

Bargains usually don't work out too well. Often the bargain roots, corms, and bulbs that are offered at the end of a season are of inferior quality or have deteriorated from poor storage. Generally speaking, you get what you pay for in buying plants. This is not to say that bargains do not sometimes appear. However, be sure you know what you're buying when you purchase.

Buy early in the season from your local nursery. Go see what your nursery has to offer, talk to the salesperson about the plants, decide what you want, and bring the plants home in the car. You should save some money by transporting them yourself.

If, however, your local nursery doesn't have what you want in stock, you will have to purchase by mail. Almost all reliable mail-order nurseries ship at the proper planting time for your particular area. Again, order as early in the season as possible so that you will not have to make substitutions for stock which is not available.

If you decide that you want specific colors or varieties which are listed, be sure to specify that you want field-grown clumps or container-grown plants. Some varieties which are particularly difficult to transplant should always be bought in containers. Also state whether or not you will accept alternate choices. If you do not wish alternates, be sure to specify "no substitutions." Also check on planting dates in your area with your local nursery and state these dates on your order. Finally, keep a copy of your order.

Prepare the ground thoroughly before your plants arrive. When they do arrive, uncover their tops but keep their roots in the packing material. Moisten the roots if they appear dry. If you should have to wait for a while before planting them, heel them in or put them in pots of soil. Water them and place them in a protected area until you are ready to plant them. Do not let the roots dry out or permit them to become water-soaked. Check your order against your list. Check for quality. If plants have been damaged in transit, write immediately to the mail-order house. Very often guarantees are not honored unless you write immediately.

Selecting Plants

Never buy cheap plants from unreliable sources. They almost always prove disappointing. Often they are old, spent stock, or they may be immature or unnamed varieties. Go to a good nursery or reliable mail-order house and order only top-quality plants. These specialists offer the best varieties of a wide range of stock.

Planting Your Garden

Take your time! Don't hurry this job, since it must be done right. First, spread a large piece of canvas or plastic on the lawn and spread your plants on it. This will save you cleanup time. A bushel basket for debris also saves time and steps. Make the holes big enough to permit the roots to grow normally. Check the instructions for each plant. Plan on planting each plant one-half to one inch deeper than the soil mark on your specimen to allow for the soil settling around the roots. Then, firm the soil around the plant or the bulbs so that there are no air pockets underneath. Be sure to start out with your tall-growing perennials, the backbone of your garden.

This border of perennial flowers, planted around a garden house, features phlox and day lilies for summer.

Now check each plant's individual soil needs. If a plant likes an alkaline soil, mix in the proper amount of lime. If your plant needs a good deal of humus or organic matter, mix it into the soil. Check off each plant as it is planted. If you see something in your original plan that is drastically wrong, change it now. Make the change on your sketch.

Place stakes or labels near each plant to identify it. This is particularly important when you plant bulbs, since the foliage doesn't appear until spring and then disappears shortly after. For your filler groups, trace the shapes with a trowel on the soil surface. Then lay out your plants and set them in the ground. Step back and look at them. If the arrangement meets with your approval, plant them. Then plant your edging plants. After you have completed your planting, thoroughly water each plant. A weak solution of soluble fertilizer may be used to encourage root growth. When you first set out your plants, protect those whose foliage wilts badly. Cover them with a basket for a few days so that the roots can absorb the moisture the plant needs to revive the foliage.

About a week after you have planted your border, cultivate it with a hoe or cultivator to the depth of one inch. This uproots the young weeds and allows the soil to receive more moisture.

Transplanting

When your plants begin to crowd, which should happen about every fourth to sixth year, you may want to redesign, remake, or replant a section. You can stagger this work by doing one section one year and another the following. Early spring or early October are the best times to do this. Plants that resent being moved or do not need replanting can be left in place. Other plants can be lifted and split. When you do this, discard the woody centers and replant only what you need to fill the spaces. Be sure to enrich the soil. At the same time, you can discard plants that you do not particularly like and try new varieties in their place.

Heliotrope is an old-fashioned annual grown for its hauntingly fragrant flowers; treat as Lobelia.

3
Annuals

An annual is a plant that completes its entire life cycle in one year—living from the sowing of the seed to the setting of the new seed at the end of the season. It dies naturally within twelve months. There are many plants that, although not technically true annuals, can be treated as such. Simply start them indoors before the outdoor planting season, nurture them, and then when the soil has warmed up, plant them outdoors to flower during the summer and die in the fall.

Annuals are perhaps the most versatile flowers that exist. They can be used to fill in gaps left after the spring bulbs and perennials have bloomed, and they can be used in hanging baskets, in window boxes, in tubs and planters, in borders, as edging, for cutting, and as fillers in new foundation plantings. In short, they are quick and easy to grow and provide a maximum of bloom with a minimum of expense and effort. Some are almost infallible.

How to Start Your Annual Garden

After the winter holidays are over, in January, you will notice advertisements in the newspapers and magazines for seed catalogs. Most of them are yours for the asking. Fill in the coupons and send for them. Then, during the bleak months of winter, peruse the catalogs and decide which seeds you want. Generally, the selection from the seed catalogs is far more extensive than that from your local nursery, supermarket, or hardware store. Make your selections and order your seeds. If you are a novice, be careful not to order more packages of seed than you can care for. A good rule of thumb is to make your selections and then cut your list in half.

Two Kinds of Annuals

Generally, there are two kinds of annuals: those that can be planted directly outdoors in spring and those that must be started in February or early March indoors. If you do not wish to start the early varieties indoors, stick to those that can be planted directly outdoors when the soil has warmed up. There are many to choose from that provide you with a bountiful blooming season later in the summer. Some *must* be started indoors (stock, wax begonia, lobelia, verbena, etc.), while others can either be started indoors or can be sown directly outdoors later.

An Alternative

These days, most nurseries offer minipacks of annuals ready to set out in the garden at the appropriate time of the spring season. Although the challenge of gardening from scratch is not involved, a great deal of work and time can be saved by purchasing these minipacks. Again, if you seek some of the more esoteric varieties of annuals, you probably won't find them here.

Planting Annual Seeds Directly Outdoors

The following instructions apply to most annuals. Annual seeds are generally small in size, so the soil must be properly prepared. First, turn the soil over with a spade to a depth of eight to ten inches. Be sure to bury any weeds growing on the surface.

When digging a plot for a flower bed, first make a shallow trench or ditch about one foot wide and about ten inches deep at one end of the area. Place the soil removed from the trench in a heap at the other end of the bed being prepared. When the plot has been completely dug, this heap of soil will be ready to fill in the last trench you dig.

Next, turn over a six-inch strip of soil bordering the trench, shoveling it forward and at the same time turning it over, so that both surface soil and weeds are buried. Continue this process until you reach the end of the bed, when the heap of soil first dug is used to fill in the last trench.

While you are digging, place a pailful of compost or well-rotted manure into the ditch before you fill it in. Do this at the rate of about one pailful per running yard of trench. Level off the bed with the spade.

Rake the surface as finely as possible just before sowing your seeds. Remove all rocks and stones from the soil and then break down all of the lumps of earth with your rake. If you have

prepared your bed in advance and have raked before, do it again before you sow your seeds.

If you live in an area where the soil is known to be acidic (check with your local nursery about this), you may have to add some agricultural lime as a dressing. Although most annuals are not that fussy about acidic soil, some, like candytuft, clearly prefer a nearly neutral or alkaline soil for best performance.

When to Sow

Most annuals which are reasonably quick growing can be sown outdoors when the weather has warmed up. A good indication of this is the leafing out of your trees. Some of the hardiest may be sown outdoors in the fall, with germination taking place in the spring. Generally, two successive sowings of each variety assure continuous bloom throughout the summer and into the fall.

Broadcast Sowing for Beds

After you have prepared your bed, as instructed above, take a stick and mark out large, informally shaped drifts or areas where the plants are to flower. Place a label in each area bearing the name of the flowers to be planted. Keep in mind that your garden plan should consider pleasant color combinations, foliage contrasts, and plant size and height. Beds to be viewed from all sides (so-called "island beds") can be planned with taller types in the middle and with intermediate and smaller edging plants falling in front of them on all sides. Sow the seeds of all varieties in a broadcast manner within their specific areas and cover the seeds so that they are just barely buried. Leave your outlines in place.

You can achieve the same effect in a bed by sowing the seeds in little shallow trenches, spaced some six to twelve inches apart, within the boundaries of each area. After you have sown the seeds, cover them with soil.

Sowing the Cutting Garden

To plant a garden primarily for cut flowers or for a border, select an area away from the house where appearance is not too important.

One of the chief reasons for growing lots of annuals is to have plenty for cutting. Here the casual bouquet consists of cosmos, petunias, zinnias, snapdragons, Queen Anne's lace and larkspur.

Make rows about one foot to one and a half feet apart in a prepared bed. This makes it easy to hoe for weeds later in the season and allows your plants plenty of room for growth. Plant four rows of seeds and allow a two-foot path. The path allows you to cut your flowers conveniently. Then plant another four rows of seeds and make another row two feet wide for a cutting path. Continue this until you have planted the entire bed. Cover seeds as described above.

Watering Newly Planted Seeds

Sprinkle your flower bed with a fine spray from the hose or with a watering can after you have planted your seeds. Check the bed each day to be sure that the soil has not dried out. If it has, water again with a fine spray.

Thinning Out Seedlings

In a week or so, after your seedlings have germinated, check to see how tall they are. Check again each day. When a seedling reaches the height of about one inch, thin out the area. Smaller plants should be thinned to four inches apart, medium-sized plants from six to nine inches apart, and very large plants from one to two feet apart. At the same time, pull out any weeds that have grown. If you sow your seeds in the fall, it is better to wait until early spring to thin them out.

Staking

As your plants grow, check each variety of the medium- and tall-growing types. Those with thin or floppy stems need staking. Do this by inserting twigs in the bed at about eight-inch intervals after the seedlings have grown about three inches tall. Some of the tall-growing varieties need more sturdy support. Tall marigolds, snapdragons, tall asters, sunflowers, and zinnias grow better and provide a better display if they are staked with sturdy bamboo.

Care During the Season

There are three simple rules to follow to assure maximum growth and blooming. First, keep your garden weed-free. You can do this with a mulch of straw, grass clippings, shredded leaves, or any of the commercially available preparations. Water your garden thoroughly during dry spells and pick off blossoms as they fade.

Annual asters make superb garden and cut flowers.

List of Annuals

Below is a list of the most popular annuals grown in America. Follow the instructions, and you will almost assuredly have very good results.

African Daisy
(Also Called Arctotis)

Season: Blooms from summer until fall.

Description: Brilliant yellow, pink, violet, or rose daisy-type flowers with attractive gray, woolly foliage.

Uses: Excellent for beds, borders, and cutting.

Culture: Sow seed indoors in the spring and pack down soil; sow outdoors when weather has warmed. Or sow directly outdoors when ground has warmed up. Thin to one foot apart.

Light: Likes full sun.

Soil: Will grow in average or poor soil as long as drainage is reasonable.

Tips: Do not fertilize, since this plant prefers a soil that is not rich. Standing water around the roots will probably kill them. Remove faded blooms to lengthen display. Resists summer heat and drought especially well.

Ageratum
(Also Called Flossflower)

Season: Blooms from June to October.

Description: Tassellike blue, white, or pink flowers in dense heads on tidy mounding-type plants. Available in both dwarf and one-foot-high varieties.

Uses: Excellent for edging the garden, especially in its dwarf form. Standard size may be used for beds, borders, rock gardens, pots, and cutting.

Culture: Sow seed indoors or in the greenhouse in early spring and harden off; plant outdoors when weather has warmed. Or sow seed outdoors when soil warms up. Thin to nine inches apart.

Light: Likes full sun.

Soil: Prefers average soil with good drainage.

Tips: First frost kills it. Subject to white-fly infestation. To combat this, apply nicotine or rotenone frequently. Remove faded flowers to lengthen display.

Alyssum

Season: Blooms from early summer until fall.

Description: Dainty, fragrant violet, rose, or white flowers with low-growing gray foliage. Varieties range from three to nine inches high.

Uses: Excellent for edging the garden or for rock gardens, pots, and window boxes.

Culture: Sow seed in spring after soil has warmed up in place where they are to grow. Thin to three inches apart.

Light: Likes full sun.

Soil: Any soil will do.

Tips: Easy to grow and quick blooming.

Anchusa
(Also Called Summer Forget-me-not)

Season: Blooms from early summer to fall.

Description: Clusters of blue or white forget-me-not-type flowers with bold foliage. Ranges in height from nine to eighteen inches.

Uses: Good for borders, window boxes, and cutting.

Culture: Sow seed in spring where plants are to bloom. Thin to six inches apart.

Light: Likes full sun.

Soil: Prefers well-drained soil.

Tips: Easy to grow and quick blooming. Most popular is all-American winner "Blue Bird" with clear, gentian-blue flowers and white eyes. Remove faded flowers to lengthen display.

Aster
(Also Called Callistephus)

Season: From midsummer until frost.

Description: The range is vast. Flowers are red, pink, purple, blue and white; single and double; varying in size from miniature to six inches across.

Uses: Ideal as bedding plants, with dwarf varieties good for edging. Good for cutting.

Culture: For best results start indoors about six weeks before last-expected heavy frost. Plant outdoors the recommended distance apart for the variety you have grown.

Light: Likes full sun, but a relentless baking sun will dry it out prematurely.

Soil: Prefers rich soil.

Tips: One of the most popular of all annuals.

Particularly good for fall gardens. Be sure not to plant in the same place two years in succession.

Baby's Breath
(Also Called Gypsophila)

Season: Blooms from mid-June until fall.

Description: Dainty, attractive, white flowers on plants with one and a half-foot-high gray stems and fine foliage.

Uses: Good for beds and cutting. Dwarf varieties useful in rock gardens.

Culture: Sow seed early in spring where plants are to bloom. Thin to six inches apart.

Light: Likes an open, sunny place.

Soil: Any soil will do.

Tips: Very easy to grow. Make successive plantings every two weeks for a continuous supply of flowers. Combines well with almost all flowers.

Bachelor's Button
(Also Called Cornflower or Centaurea)

Season: Blooms from June to September.

Description: Attractive blue, purple, white, or pink thistlelike flowers in close heads blossom on these two and a half-foot-high upright-growing, branched plants.

Uses: Good for beds and cutting.

Culture: Sow seed in early spring where plants are to bloom. Thin to nine inches apart. Plant every two weeks for a succession of bloom.

Light: Likes full sun, although will bloom in light shade.

Soil: Any soil will do.

Tips: Very easy to grow. Remove faded flowers to lengthen display. Otherwise, plants tend to bloom themselves to death and become unsightly by midsummer.

Balsam
(Also Called Ladyslipper
and Impatiens Balsamina)

Season: Blooms from midsummer to fall.

Description: Double and semidouble one and a half-inch blooms in a wide range of colors grow along the stems. Available in tall, two and a half-foot and ten-inch dwarf, varieties.

Uses: Old-fashioned bedding favorite.

Culture: Sow outdoors when danger of frost is over. Thin to nine inches apart.

Light: Likes sun, although will thrive in light shade.

Soil: Likes rich, slightly moist, well-drained soil but does well in lesser conditions.

Tips: Very easy to grow. Reseeds itself readily.

Begonia
(Also Called Wax Begonia)

Season: Early summer until frost.

Description: Mounds of white, pink, and scarlet flowers on green- or bronze-colored foliage. Neat compact growth from six to nine inches in height.

Uses: Ideal for summer borders and edging. Good for window boxes and pot culture.

Culture: Sow seeds indoors in January and February. Set them outside after frost some eight to twelve inches apart.

Light: Thrives in sun and light shade as well.

Soil: Most any soil will do.

Tips: Nearly pest-free and rarely harmed by wind or heavy rain. If watered regularly, resists very hot weather. Can be placed in pots during the fall and grown indoors during the winter.

Brachycome
(Also Called Swan River Daisy)

Season: Blooms from July until fall.

Description: Daisy-like flowers of white, blue, lilac, and rose bloom on a dense foliage carpet about nine inches tall. Fragrant.

Uses: Excellent for pots, rock gardens, or edgings.

Culture: Sow indoors in early spring, harden off; plant outdoors after soil has warmed up. For slightly later bloom, plant in the open when weather is warm.

Light: Likes sun or light shade.

Soil: Ordinary soil will do.

Tips: Very easy to grow.

Calendula
(Also Called Pot Marigold)

Season: Blooms from midsummer until fall.

Description: Colorful yellow, orange, and apricot blooms on upright, brittle plants growing over two feet tall. Single and double varieties available. Unique fragrance.

Uses: Good for bedding and cutting.

Culture: In mild climates, sow in September for early summer bloom. In colder climates sow in early spring for flowers from July through frost. Thin to nine inches apart.

Light: Likes full sun.

Soil: Not fussy about soil.

Tips: Easy to grow. Remove faded heads to lengthen display.

California Poppy

Season: Blooms from June to fall.

Description: Vivid flowers of orange, red, and pink which bloom on finely cut, blue-green leaves. About eighteen inches high with a spreading habit.

Uses: Good for informal edging, in rock gardens, or on sunny banks.

Culture: Sow seed in early spring where plants are to grow. Thin to six inches apart. For early bloom, sow in fall.

Light: Prefers sunny location.

Soil: Likes poor, sandy soil.

Tips: Easy to grow. Can become a nuisance plant under certain conditions, since flowers resow themselves prolifically.

Candytuft
(Also Called Annual Iberis)

Season: Blooms from early summer to fall.

Description: White, red, purple, and lilac blooms on compact, low-growing foliage.

Uses: Good for edging, rock gardens, and walls.

Culture: Sow in early spring where plants are to bloom. Thin to six inches apart.

Light: Likes sun.

Soil: Prefers light, well-drained soil.

Tips: Easy to grow. Sow every two or three weeks for successive bloom. Reseeds itself in subsequent years.

Carnation

Season: Midsummer until frost.

Description: Beautifully fringed, fully double flowers scented sweetly with clove. Grows to eighteen inches.

Uses: Excellent in borders and for cutting.

Culture: Sow seeds indoors six weeks before last expected frost. Plant outdoors after weather has warmed. Place twelve to eighteen inches apart according to variety selected. (Taller varieties should be placed further apart.)

Light: Likes full sun.

Soil: Prefers rich soil.

Tips: When buds form, pinch all but one from each stem to encourage larger blooms.

Clarkia

Season: Blooms from midsummer to fall.

Description: Flowers are purple, rose, clear pink, salmon, and white. They bloom on bush plants one to three feet tall.

Uses: Useful in mixed borders or in cutting gardens, since flowers last well.

Culture: Sow in April in well-drained soil. Thin to six inches apart.

Light: Likes sun or light shade.

Soil: Prefers well-drained, fertilized, slightly acidic soil.

Tips: Good cutting flower *if* placed in water immediately after picking. Does not fare well in localities where the summers are oppressively hot and humid.

Wax begonia will bloom in sun or shade.

Cleome
(Also Called Spider Plant)

Season: Blooms from early summer to fall.

Description: Very attractive, tall, weather-resistant plant with huge trusses of bloom in rose, purple, lilac, pink, and white set in lobed foliage.

Uses: Good for backgrounds, accents, and cutting.

Culture: Sow seed indoors in early spring and set out eighteen inches apart when weather has warmed up. Or for slightly later bloom, sow directly outdoors in spring after soil has warmed.

Light: Likes sun.

Soil: Prefers light, sandy soil.

Tips: Even though this plant grows from three to six feet tall, the stems are stalwart and do not need to be staked.

Cockscomb
(Also Called Celosia)

Season: Blooms from midsummer until fall.

Description: Old-fashioned plants that grow between nine inches and two feet in height. Much improvement has been made in currently available varieties. Individual flowers are tiny but are borne on plumed, flattened, or spiked clusters of red, yellow, pink, and rose. Leaves are bronze colored or red margined.

Uses: Useful for massed bedding because of its rather stiff, formal appearance. Also useful for cutting and for drying for winter bouquets.

Culture: Easy to grow if sown in the open ground after the soil has warmed up. May also be started indoors in March for earlier blooming and then set outdoors when weather has warmed.

Light: Likes sun.

Soil: Prefers light textured but rich soil with plenty of moisture.

Tips: Worst enemy is red spider. Hose down daily during midsummer with clear water.

Plumosa

This is a variety of cockscomb. Showy, well-branched plants are crowned with silky, feathery plumes. Follow the procedures for cockscomb.

Coleus

Season: Reaches maturity by July and lasts until fall.

Description: Does not have flowers but does have colorful leaves of amber, brown, bronze, scarlet, green, and rich mahogany crimson. Grown for its foliage.

Uses: Excellent for pots, window boxes, and edging.

Culture: Sow in spring after ground has warmed up and thin to six inches.

Light: Likes sun or light shade.

Soil: Ordinary soil.

Tips: Comes in standard fifteen-inch height (Rainbow) and in dwarf eight-inch height (Carefree).

Coreposis
(Also Called Calliopsis)

Season: Blooms from early summer to frost.

Description: Gay, daisylike flowers of yellow, orange, red, maroon, and crimson. Eight-inch to four-foot-high plants with attractive foliage. Wiry stems carry blooms singly or in clusters.

Uses: Good for borders and cutting. Some compact varieties look well in rock gardens or as edging plants.

Culture: Sow seed in fall where winters are mild or in spring elsewhere. Sow where plants are to bloom. Thin to nine inches apart.

Light: Likes sun.

Soil: Grows well in ordinary soil.

Tips: Very easy to grow. Very tolerant of poor soil, summer heat, and drought. Prolific bloomers.

Cosmo

Season: Blooms from early summer to frost.

Description: Bright clear red, rose, pink, yellow, white, and crimson disclike flowers on three- to six-foot-high plants with feathery foliage.

Uses: Good for cover over early bulbs or for filler between early flowering plants or as tall background material for the annual border. Also good as cut flower.

Culture: Start indoors in early spring. Or sow where they are to grow after danger of frost is over.

Thin to eighteen inches apart.

This Cyclone impatiens hybrid has creamy white leaves edged in green and vivid orange flowers all summer.

Light: Likes sun.

Soil: Rich soil is not required, but it should be well-drained.

Tips: Pinch when plant is about one foot high to encourage branching and bushier plants. Reseeds readily.

Dianthus
(Also Called Annual Pink)

Season: Blooms from midsummer until frost.

Description: Brilliant-colored flowers of scarlet, salmon, white, and crimson shades that grow on tidy, attractive eight- to twelve-inch-high plants. Clove fragrance.

Uses: Excellent for garden decoration and cutting.

Culture: Sow seed indoors early in season, transplant, and harden off; plant outdoors as soon as danger of frost is past. Or for later bloom, sow directly outdoors in spring. Thin from six to eight inches apart.

Light: Grows best in full sun but will do reasonably well in light shade.

Soil: Prefers well-drained, neutral or slightly alkaline soil.

Tips: In areas with mild winters, often winters over and blooms the following year.

Hollyhock

Season: Blooms in midsummer.

Description: Tall plants, five to nine feet high, with flowers arranged in terminal spikes or racemes. Flowers are saucer-shaped; single, double, or frilled; in shades of maroon, red, pink, yellow, salmon, or white.

Uses: Can be used wherever tall, stately plants will be seen to good advantage. Particularly good at the back of perennial borders. Can also be used effectively against fences, walls, and houses. Particularly effective against old colonial houses.

Culture: Plant annual varieties in spring after danger of heavy frost has passed. Hollyhocks do not move well when they are mature, so be sure to plant them where you want them to grow.

Light: Likes sun but will bloom in light shade.

Soil: Prefers a deep rich soil but will grow in ordinary soil.

Tips: Self-sows readily.

Impatiens
(Also Called Sultan's Balsam, Touch-me-not, and Patience Plant)

Season: Blooms from midsummer until frost.

Description: Recent developments in horticulture have vastly expanded the available varieties. Colors range from white through many shades of orange, salmon, red, pink, and purple. Single and double varieties are available as well as bicolored offerings. Standard and dwarf varieties available. Bright flowers one to two inches across grow on deep-green handsome foliage.

Uses: Excellent for beds in the shade, borders, pots, tubs, or planter boxes. Also serves as a house plant in the winter.

Culture: Start indoors six to eight weeks before last expected frost and harden off. Plant outdoors when weather has warmed.

Light: Thrives in medium shade. One of the best plants to brighten up a shady nook in the garden.

Soil: Prefers ordinary soil that is not excessively dry.

Tips: As mentioned above, one of the few flowers that truly thrives in the shade.

Larkspur
(Also Called Annual Delphinium)

Season: Blooms in midsummer.

Description: Erect, branching plant, three to four feet high with large spikes of blue, red, white, and purple flowers.

Uses: Excellent as cut flowers, especially Giant Imperial and Giant Steeplechase varieties. Use as a background for annual borders or as specimen plants in borders.

Culture: Easily grown *except* that it is fussy about temperatures during germination period. Therefore, seeds must be sown very early in the spring about the same time that peas are sown or in the fall, with germination taking place in the spring.

Light: Grows best in full sun.

Soil: Prefers moderately rich, well-drained soil. Well-rotted manure worked into the soil helps them attain maximum growth and flower display.

Tips: Although the blooming period is short, larkspur is so spectacular that it is worth planting.

Lobelia

Season: Blooms from early summer to fall.

Description: Low, bushy, four-inch-high plants with intense French-blue flowers with white eyes and white, maroon, or light-blue flowers. Also trailing varieties.

Uses: Good for edging. One of the few plants that do well in partial shade. Trailing varieties are spectacular in hanging baskets.

Culture: Sow indoors in early spring. Seedlings are very small, so when transplanting outdoors after danger of frost is over, plant in bunches some four to six inches apart.

Light: Thrives in partial shade or in sun.

Soil: Prefers moist soil but also thrives in ordinary soils.

Tips: In hot, sunny climates, grows better in shade.

Marigold
(Also Called Friendship Flower)

Season: Blooms from early summer until frost.

Description: An almost incredible number of

varieties available (see chart below). Colors include yellow, orange, bronze, and bicolors.

Uses: Almost anything. Beds, borders, edging, baskets, pots, window boxes, and cutting.

Culture: Sow seeds indoors in spring and harden off; plant outdoors after frost. Or sow directly outdoors after danger of frost has passed. Thin to distance recommended for your variety.

Light: Marigolds like sun but will bloom in partial shade.

Soil: Ordinary soil will do.

Tips: In 1976, after many years of quest, a white marigold was discovered. It will be offered to the public soon by Burpee Seeds. Truly America's most popular annual and with good reason: it rarely fails to perform magnificently and is extremely easy to grow.

Nasturtium
(Also Called Indian Cress)

Season: Blooms from midsummer until fall.

Description: Fragrant, funnellike flowers in single or double form in many colors of the yellow, orange, and red range with rounded dark-green leaves. Compact varieties as well as climbers.

Uses: Useful as border plant with climbers

Marigolds

First Lady marigold.

Variety	Height	Flower	Comments
Petite Gold	6"	Fully double 1¼" golden flowers on compact mounds.	Petite series. French type. Series also includes Petite Orange, Petite Yellow, and Petite Mix.
Petite Spry	7"	Double red with yellow crest.	
Petite Harmony	8"	Mahogany red and orange.	
Brownie Scout	8"	Fully double 1¼". Gold splashed with red.	French type with petite-mound habit.
Lemon Drop	6–8"	Fully double 1¼" lemon yellow.	Petite-mound habit.
Yellow Nugget	10–12"	Double 2¼" flowers.	Nugget series. Also includes Orange Nugget, Gold Nugget, and mixed colors.
Pumpkin Crush	10–12"	Huge, fully double 4½" orange blooms.	Guys and Dolls series. Also offered as yellow, gold, and mixed varieties.
Aztec	10–12"	Gold, yellow, orange mix 3–4" flowers.	Double carnation type.
Bolero	10–12"	Fully double 2½" flowers. Bright maroon, gold center.	Double French bicolor.
Honeycomb	10–12"	Fully double 1½" crested blooms. Maroon petals, gold border.	Royal Crested series, also includes the bicolors: "Autumn Haze," "Gold Rush," and "Star Dust."
Gold Cupid	10–12"	Mumlike 2½" blooms.	Cupid series includes: orange, yellow, and mix varieties.
Spanish Brocade	10–12"	Gold and deep red blooms.	Semidouble French bicolor. Very early.

and in window boxes, trellises, or banks. Flowers good for cutting.

Culture: Sow outdoors after frost. Thin to six or eight inches apart.

Light: Likes sunny or lightly shaded spot.

Soil: Grows in ordinary soil

Tips: Pungent foliage is very good in salads. Flowers and seeds can be pickled. Rich soil produces vigorous foliage but few blooms.

Nicotiana
(Also Called Tobacco Plant)

Season: Blooms from midsummer until fall.

Description: Large, fast-growing plants with long tubular flowers. Predominantly white, but also red, pink, yellow and purple.

Uses: Useful as fillers in the border after the bulbs have bloomed.

Culture: Sow seed indoors in early spring or outdoors after weather has warmed. Thin to eighteen inches apart.

Light: Requires sun, although some blooms will appear on plants grown in shade.

Soil: Average soil is required.

Tips: Very fragrant with a tobacco smell. Some varieties bloom at night and combine well against a trellis of moonflower vines, which also bloom at night. Self-sows readily.

Fiesta	12″	Carnation type crimson and yellow.	Olé series includes Matador and Picador.
Tiger	12–15″	Closely packed petals of bright gold.	A triploid hybrid with extra-long flowering period. Earliest of the group.
Showboat	13″	2½″ golden yellow.	Triploid hybrid.
Harvest Moon	14″	Crested 1½″ blooms.	Moon series also includes Honey, Honey Moon (yellow). Blooms at 6″.
Rusty Red	14″	Well-doubled 2½″ rusty mahogany blooms.	Becomes marked with gold as it matures.
Gold Galore	14–16″	Double carnation type 3¼″ golden yellow.	Densely branched, compact bush.
First Lady	18″	Double carnation type 3¼″ yellow.	Lady series. Also includes Gold Lady and Orange Lady. Hedge type. Erect, bushy rounded.
Naughty Marietta	18–20″	2″ single golden yellow with red eye.	Also in this class is Dainty Marietta, lower growing to 12″.
Senator Dirksen	24″	Double carnation-type 3½″ golden yellow.	Hedge type. Very vigorous. Have grown to 34″.
Orange Hawaii	30–36″	Double carnation-type 4″ blooms.	Odorless foliage. Carnation flowered. Series includes Golden Hawaii.
Yellow Crackerjack	30–36″	Double carnation-type 5″ blooms.	Crackerjack series. Also offered as orange, gold, and mix. Erect, busy.
Yellow Doubloon	36″	Extra-double carnation-type 3½″–4″ blooms.	Gold Coin series. Also includes Sovereign (gold) and Double Eagle (orange).
Yellow Climax	36″	Fully double carnation-type 5″ ruffled, globular blooms.	Climax series includes Golden, Primrose, Toreador, and mix. Sturdy, erect, and bushy.

Dwarf hybrid nasturtiums.

Petunia

Season: Early summer until frost.

Description: Dozens of new varieties are offered with blooms ranging from one to three and a half inches in diameter. Colors run the gamut from red, pink, salmon, and crimson to blue, purple, white, and yellow. There are bushy types and trailing types, ranging in height from twelve to fifteen inches.

Uses: Extremely versatile. Used in beds, borders, pots, window boxes, and baskets.

Culture: Start seed indoors from late January through mid-March and harden off; plant outside after danger of frost has passed. Plant one foot apart.

Light: Likes sun.

Soil: Prefers well-drained, slightly acid soil.

Tips: Tends to become straggly toward midsummer unless properly pruned. Be sure to pinch faded blossoms. Don't let plant go to seed or display will fade.

Phlox

Season: Blooms from midsummer until fall.

Description: Plant grows eighteen inches high, erect, with many branches topped with clusters of flowers in shades from buff, pink, salmon, red, and purple to brilliant orange. Dwarf varieties are seven inches tall.

Uses: Beautiful for bedding, used in a mixed border, and for cutting. Dwarf varieties are particularly good for pots and window boxes.

Culture: Sow in spring outdoors when soil has warmed up. Thin to nine inches apart.

Light: Likes a sunny place.

Soil: Prefers slightly acid soil but does well in ordinary soil as well.

Tips: Easy to grow, wide color range. Remove faded flowers for continuous bloom.

Portulaca
(Also Called Rose Moss or Sun Rose)

Season: Blooms from early summer until frost.

Description: Newer varieties are great improvements on the traditional portulaca. Large double flowers in a rainbow of colors smother slow-growing fleshy plants.

Uses: Excellent for low borders and rock gardens. Forms a thick, dense carpet.

Culture: Sow seed in spring after danger of frost in place where plants are to grow. Thin to three or four inches apart.

Light: Likes full sun.

Soil: Prefers dry, poor soil

Tips: This is a perfect plant for those places where nothing seems to grow. Also good at the seashore. Flowers close on dull days and on bright days close around noon. Often reseeds itself.

Salpiglossis
(Also Called Painted Tongue or Velvet Flower)

Season: Blooms early summer to frost.

Description: Velvety flowers are funnel-shaped with a wide throat and come in red, purple, brown, yellow, and cream. They are veined with gold.

Uses: Grow in the mixed border, annual, or cutting garden.

Culture: Must have an early start in order to perform satisfactorily. Start seed indoors in February so that plant has good growth before planting outside, nine inches apart after danger of frost.

Light: Prefers sun.

Soil: Likes rich soil.

Tips: Remove faded blooms for continuous bloom. Often self-sows.

Salvia
(Also Called Sage)

Season: Blooms from midsummer until fall.

Description: Very brilliant flowers in various red colors on many-stemmed plants growing from one and a half to four feet high.

Uses: Excellent for beds, borders, edgings, and pot culture.

Culture: Sow indoors about eight weeks before last-expected spring frost. Set plants in garden when soil is warm. Thin to eight inches apart.

Light: Will grow in sun or light shade.

Soil: Requires only ordinary soil with good drainage.

Tips: When plants are three to four inches high, pinch tips to encourage branching. Seeds sown directly in the garden after frost will not bloom until mid-August. A very showy plant.

Dwarf asters, medium-size marigolds and tall snapdragons.

Be very careful to avoid planting it where its vivid colors would clash with or overwhelm more delicate and subtle flowers.

Scabiosa
(Also Called Pincushion Flower)
Season: Blooms from midsummer until fall.

Description: Upright, bushy plants. Often weedy in habit. Flowers resemble pincushions and are colored white, cream, dark red, and various shades of blue and lavender.

Uses: Good for cutting. Weedy habit does not lend itself particularly to bedding.

Culture: Sow seeds in early April where plants are to flower. Thin to three or four inches apart.

Light: Likes sun.

Soil: Prefers light soil.

Tips: Some people like them, but frankly you'll do better with other varieties of annuals.

Snapdragons
(Also Called Antirrhinum)
Season: Blooms from early summer to frost.

Description: The color range is vast with many varieties. Single, double, and butterfly available. Flower spikes rise directly from the crown. Heights range from six to eight inches to five feet or more.

Uses: Absolutely beautiful in borders and for backgrounds. The smaller varieties are excellent for bedding and edging. Superb cut flower.

Culture: Sow seed indoors early in the spring and transplant seedlings into flats, two inches apart when they are three inches tall. Pinch out the tip to encourage branching. Plant outdoors when danger from frost has passed.

Light: Likes full sun, but will bloom reasonably in partial shade.

Soil: Prefers a fairly rich, well-drained soil, slightly on the alkaline side. If soil is acidic, add a little ground limestone when you prepare the bed.

Tips: Often winters over in moderate climates. Usually, the second year's blooming is even more spectacular than the first. A must for any flower garden.

Stock
(Also Called Mathiola or Gillflower)
Season: Blooms from midsummer until a killing frost, often as late as December in the Northeast.

Description: Single or double flowers in a wide color range including white, rose, red, purple, pale yellow, and apricot. Very fragrant. The foliage is sturdy and erect, growing to two and a half feet high.

Uses: Good for bedding and cutting.

Culture: Start seeds indoors early in the spring and harden off; plant outside after danger of frost. Grows best during the cool days and evenings of early spring.

Light: Likes sun but can tolerate some shade.

Soil: Prefers a rich, deep, well-manured soil.

Tips: In milder climates, winters over and blooms in subsequent years. Grown primarily as a cut flower and for its fragrance.

Sunflower
(Also Called Helianthus)
Season: Blooms from July through September.

Description: Very tall, single-stalk stems bearing immense yellow flowers with brown centers.

Uses: Spectacular as a background for a garden. The seeds are relished by birds and can be dried at the end of the season and stored for winter use. People also like to eat them.

Culture: Sow seed in spring where plants are to flower. Thin out to two feet apart.

Verbena is an outstanding annual for growing in a hot, dry, sunny place. Here it grows among large rocks.

Light: Likes full sun.

Soil: Ordinary soil will do.

Tips: May grow to ten feet. Has no place in a general annual border. Plant against a fence or use as a sun screen.

Sweet Pea
(Also Called Lathyrus)

Season: Blooms from late spring to midsummer. In colder areas may bloom until fall. Vines do not grow well in hot weather and cannot stand drought.

Description: Fragrant, pealike flowers in the complete color range grow on tendril climbing vines, which may reach five feet. Some bush-type varieties are also available.

Uses: Excellent as a cut flower. Bush varieties can be bedded. Climbing varieties can be trained on trellises or used to hide unsightly compost piles, etc.

Culture: Plant in March in the North. In less severe climates, plant in the fall. Thin to eight inches apart.

Light: Needs full sun.

Soil: Prepare soil with well-rotted manure and other organic matter to a depth of eighteen inches. Some bone meal and ground limestone should also be added.

Bijou sweet pea is an excellent choice for a window box.

Portulaca is great for flowers in a hot, sunny, dry spot.

Tips: Cut spent flowers to prolong bloom. Provide brush, string, or netting for climbing varieties. Involves some work, but the rewards are great.

Torenia
(Also Called Wishbone Flower)

Season: Blooms from early summer until fall.

Description: Has mauve standards, violet-blue lips, and bright-yellow blotches. Grows on eight-inch-tall compact bushy plant.

Uses: Fine for borders, pots, window boxes,

and rock gardens.

Culture: Sow seed directly outdoors after danger of frost. Thin to eight inches apart.

Light: Adapts well to light shade although prefers sun.

Soil: Ordinary soil will do.

Tips: Especially valuable for shady locations. May reseed itself.

Verbena

Season: Blooms from midsummer until fall.

Description: Colorful, dwarf plants with flowers borne in large trusses in red, pink, lilac, and white. Often fragrant, and many varieties have white eyes. Has a tendency to spread, with one plant covering a considerable amount of space by the end of the season.

Uses: Good for bedding, edgings, rock gardens, and window boxes.

Culture: Sow seed indoors and harden off; plant outdoors after danger of frost has passed. Or plant directly outdoors after weather has warmed. Thin to nine inches apart.

Light: Likes sun.

Soil: Will thrive in ordinary soil.

Tips: It is best to sow these seeds indoors early in the spring, since they do not start blooming until August when they have a late start. Easy to grow. Thrives in almost any soil.

Zinnia

Season: Blooms from midsummer until frost.

Description: Another of the most versatile flowers in existence, ranging in size from miniature to giant blooms in an extraordinary range of colors. Grows anywhere from eight inches to four feet high. Large, extravagantly showy varieties, prolific bloom, and handsome foliage make this one of the great favorites.

Uses: In borders, for edging, and for cutting.

Culture: Sow indoors before the frost is over, harden off, and plant outside. Or sow directly outdoors after danger of frost. Thin according to variety from eight to eighteen inches apart.

Light: Likes full sun.

Soil: Ordinary soil is acceptable but grows better in fertile soil.

Tips: Pinch the terminal bud or the plants will tend to produce only one flower on one stem. Pinching helps the plant to branch.

The hosta is one of the best of all perennials for handsome foliage and flowers in moist, humusy soil and part shade.

4
Perennials

The varieties of perennials offered to the gardener are almost limitless. Perennials are available in just about every height, color, and season of bloom. And they offer any gardener a fine return for the outlay of time, energy, and money. Although these plants are more expensive to buy than the general bedding annual or bedding plant, in the long run they are cheaper. Once you have planted them, they live for many years, and most of them increase dramatically. If you select a reasonably large group for your garden, they will bloom from early spring to late fall. You should plant early-blooming, mid-season, and late-flowering kinds.

Light and Air

The usual perennial borders tend to encourage weak growth. If a hedge is used as a backing, if trees or shrubs are nearby, or if the garden is over-crowded, the plants do not thrive properly. This is because light is restricted, and there is no free circulation of air. These conditions cause weak stems and encourage various diseases.

There is another disadvantage of using a conventional border treatment for your perennials. Many varieties are simply too tall for a narrow strip. If they are properly spaced in beds that receive proper light from all sides and a free flow of air, they increase in size from year to year and yet maintain their normal growing height. If a narrow strip is used with a wall, hedge, or tree background, the plants grow taller in their search for these elements. The result is leggy plants that are out of balance with the shorter plants in the garden.

Exposure

Most perennial borders face in only one direction. Since most of the hardy perennials love sun, a southern exposure should be planned if possible. If you must place your garden facing north, then use perennials that prefer partial shade. There are a large number of these to choose from, but some may be difficult to get from your local nursery. Most plant emporiums stock the more popular sun-loving plants. Keep in mind that wind, particularly one whipped up by a sudden storm or gale, can wreak havoc with your perennial garden. If you have located your border in an area that is exposed to wind, be sure to stake your plants carefully. Island beds (that is, those that can be viewed from all four sides) need less staking if set in an unenclosed area.

Soil

Most hardy perennials are not very fussy about soil. Some varieties prefer a richer or moister soil than others, but there is such a wide selection available that almost any soil situation can be accommodated. You can even have a fine perennial garden in the middle of the city. Basically, all of the perennials listed below should have well-drained soil.

A few perennials require an acidic soil; however, most will thrive in a nearly neutral soil. Generally speaking, if vegetables and annuals grow well on your land, a wide range of perennials will also grow.

Site

Try to select a site where sun and air are not restricted. And aim for the maximum width that your scheme can accommodate. A bed that is ten or twelve feet wide is not too wide. Narrower beds will be effective as well, but you must plan and select your plants more carefully. First get rid of all perennial weeds. You can do this with a chemical weed killer or by digging and removing the roots of the weeds. You can bury the weeds in the soil, but you are probably better off disposing of them elsewhere: although some will rot, others may come back even stronger than before.

Improving the Soil

For the most part, perennials do not need unusually rich soil. But mixing manure, rotting compost, or peat moss (along with bone meal or some other organic fertilizer) will give you better results in the last analysis. Do this during the preliminary preparation of the bed. If you are blessed with soil that is dark with

humus and has a good, loamy texture, fertilizer alone may give the plants the good start they need. If the soil is acidic, have a test made and correct the soil by liming. Your local nursery can fill you in on this procedure.

Traditional Borders

The traditional perennial border is almost always planted against a hedge, a row of shrubs, a wall, or a fence. The border may be straight or curved, and it may vary in width. There are disadvantages to this particular plan, but nonetheless, effective results can be attained, especially if the border is wide enough (eight feet or more). At six feet the width for plants is only three or four feet. This is not to say that you can't plan an attractive border of that width; however, the larger border is generally more effective.

If you are planting against a hedge, shrubs, or a wall, keep in mind that hedges have roots that spread some three or more feet on either side, drawing moisture and nourishment from the soil. So allow at least two feet and preferably three feet between a hedge and perennials.

Fences and walls do not take moisture from the soil, but they may affect air circulation and light. Some fences reflect heat and slowly bake the plants during the long, hot, midsummer months. So leave two to three feet in front of the wall before planting your perennials.

In a narrow border, avoid using very tall plants. Medium- and low-growing plants look better. A rule of thumb is to limit yourself to plants whose height is one-half the effective width of the border. Place the plants more or less in order of height. Short plants belong in front.

Island Beds

The advantages of island beds are that light and air are less restricted, growth is more vigorous, and the normal heights of plants are maintained, since they do not have to "stretch" to find light. If you space your plants properly and plan ahead, you can achieve near perfection most easily with this general scheme. You can plan your garden in straight lines and in formal shapes (such as ovals and oblongs) or you can plan it informally, generally following the scheme of your tree and shrubbing arrangements. Beds of this nature can also jut out into the lawn at certain places. You can plan small beds featuring only one or two kinds of plants or larger beds planted with many different varieties. This is probably the most versatile style of bedding in use today.

Mixed Beds and Borders

There are many varieties of perennials that bloom spectacularly for only a short period of time. In many parts of America where summers are hot, perennials cannot supply a continuous bloom from spring through fall. In these areas—to fill in the gaps during the early spring and hot, midsummer months—many people mix in annuals, biennials, and bulbs.

Mixed beds, if planned properly and maintained regularly, can be very effective. Keep in mind that space must be left between the various varieties of perennials to accommodate the annuals and biennials. Limit these spaces to five square feet. This is a large enough plot to fork over and fertilize each year shortly before planting time. Plan on using annuals and biennials that bloom throughout the season, not those that coincide with your perennial bloom. Some of these are marigolds, zinnias, petunias, ageratum, nicotiana, and dwarf dahlias.

Special-purpose Plantings

Midget beds or borders can also be effective in small gardens. These can be as narrow as five feet. In these small beds, utilize the hardy perennials that are normally used in rock gardens. (Hardy rock-garden perennials are also effective when used as frontal groups in small beds.) The heights of these plants range from six inches to two and a half feet, and if you are imaginative, you can achieve effects both varied and charming.

Other types of perennial gardens to consider are those that provide flowers for cutting at certain periods of the year, those that attract bees, those that are highly fragrant, and those

Delphiniums, bearded iris and pansies star in this garden.

with silver or gray variegated foliage. Others can be used as ground cover, some present a formal appearance, and still others look well between or in front of shrubs. However, in any of these arrangements, be sure to plan ahead carefully.

Season of Bloom

If you plan carefully, you should be able to achieve a border that offers some bloom throughout the entire season. Even though a border planned for spring or fall provides a spectacular show at the chosen time, most gardeners strive for maximum continuity. Some perennials bloom for several weeks, while others (such as the iris and peony) bloom only for a few weeks during the late spring. So place your plants in your scheme with continuity in mind. For example, if you are using iris, do not put all of your groups at one end of the garden. Spread them out throughout the border. Varieties that bloom early should be placed behind plants such as chrysanthemums, which become bushy as the season progresses and hide the untidy spent plant.

You can plan your garden for color contrast or for an overall effect of blended color. Keep in mind that white flowers bring harmony to colors that might otherwise tend to clash.

Spread

Some varieties of perennials (such as bee balm, phlox, and helenium) grow and spread faster than others. Use your discretion when it comes to this. The more robust kinds may grow two or three times faster than the less. If the faster growing varieties are planted adjacent to the slower, trouble may result. If your space is limited, simply leave out the fast-growing varieties.

When the second season has arrived, you can see which plants have encroached on others. Curb them ruthlessly. A good rule of thumb is that the slowest, spreading kinds of plants are most often the best bet.

How to Improve an Existing Border

If you are saddled with a border that was poorly planned in the first place, very often you can improve it. The most frequent problem is a border that is too narrow for the plants it contains, particularly for the tall plants. The light and air may have become restricted. To remedy this, simply remove the overly tall plants and replace them with shorter ones.

On the other hand, the entire border may need an overhaul with thorough spading and fertilization. Only use plants that can be adapted to the site, filling out the border with new selections.

When to Plant

Most perennials should be planted in early fall while the soil is still warm. This allows plenty of time for the roots to become established and also provides good, strong plants for spring bloom. You can also plant in the spring. In the spring, however, there may be danger from overly dry soil following planting, so be sure to keep your border well watered. There are plants which should be set out in the spring. Check with your local nursery about this and follow its instructions.

When you start planting, spade your garden, improve the soil, and select your plants. Lay out your garden and go to town. Before you set your plants out, check the soil. If it is dry, water it thoroughly and plant the following day. If the weather is dry after planting, water thoroughly with a fine spray.

When you set your plants in place, spread the roots in their natural positions and firm the soil about them. If the soil is wet and sticky, do not pack it tightly around the roots. The drier the soil, the more firmly you should pack.

During the first season be sure to water thoroughly all summer. The roots have not yet sunk deeply into the earth and need water. If you have prepared your soil properly before planting, there should be no need to fertilize.

Weed Control

You must weed your garden. Hoe annual weeds when they are small. If you have prepared your site properly, perennial weeds should not appear. If they do, dig them out. Do not use chemicals after you have planted.

Staking

Staking is a chore, no doubt, but it is necessary. Keep your staking tidy, since nothing looks worse than a garden filled with a lot of carelessly placed sticks feebly trying to support plants. Use attractive materials, such as bamboo. Plain old pieces of wood rarely look well. Place the supports in place when the plants become floppy. Use soft twine or some material that will not cut into the plant. Make the ties loose enough to allow for growth of the stems.

Fertilizing and Mulching

If you have prepared your bed properly, no fertilization is necessary during the first year. In subsequent seasons, however, add nourishment to the soil. In the early spring or in the late fall, fork in old manure and rotted compost along with an organic fertilizer. This should suffice for most varieties of plants. Delphiniums, however, in order to achieve spectacular bloom, should be very heavily fertilized each year and after they bloom.

To keep your garden weed-free and to cut down on maintenance, mulch. Use grass clippings, peat moss, buckwheat hulls, sawdust, or other mulches offered by nurseries. If you are lucky enough to have a shredder, use shredded leaves. All of these mulches eventually break down and enrich the soil.

Keeping Your Garden Watered

When the weather is dry, water to a depth of six to eight inches. Do not merely sprinkle the surface of your garden. You would do more harm than good. Deep soaking once a week is far more effective than daily sprinkles. There are hoses available which facilitate the watering process.

Winter Protection

In very cold areas of the country, provide winter protection for your garden in the form of a surface covering of salt hay, evergreen branches, or some material that permits free access of air. Most fallen leaves are not good for this purpose, since they mat down and smother the plant. When the ground freezes, plants have a tendency to "heave" to the surface. The winter cover minimizes the heaving and protects roots that may be exposed. Put this cover on your garden when the soil has frozen to a depth of two or three inches. Gradually remove it in the spring when the new growth appears.

Diseases and Pests

Specific diseases and pests are dealt with in Chapter 11. However, as a starter to prevent infestation or disease, cut down all stems and foliage killed by frost. Place this on your compost heap, or if it is diseased, burn it.

List of Perennials

A list of recommended perennials follows.

Achillea
(Also Called Yarrow and Milfoil)
Season: Blooms from June to September, depending on variety.

Description: Ground hugging or tall, erect plants of rather stiff appearance. Flowers are in heads of small clusters of yellow, white, or rose, depending on variety. Foliage on dwarf species is in woolly, gray tufts. On upright varieties, leaves are almost fernlike and are fragrant.
Uses: Dwarf varieties do well in rock gardens, while uprights are useful in borders for yellow accents.
Culture: Set out in spring or fall. Space some ten inches apart.
Light: Likes full sun.
Soil: Prefers well-drained soil.
Propagation: By division, cuttings, or seeds.
Tips: Cut flower heads off after bloom. Dries well for winter arrangements.

Aconitum
(Also Called Monkshood and Wolfsbane)
Season: Blooms in June.
Description: Most species are tall-growing delphiniumlike plants with showy flowers of blue, violet, and occasionally white. There are also some yellow and dark-red varieties.
Uses: Looks well in borders or naturalized in semiwild gardens. Good for cutting.
Culture: Plant in spring or fall from nine to twelve inches apart.
Light: Grows well in full sun or light shade.
Soil: Prefers rich, well-drained soil. Will not survive ground floods for any length of time.
Propagation: By seed or division. When divided, several years must pass before they recuperate fully.
Tips: Roots are poisonous if eaten. Care should be taken in handling them, especially if you have any cuts or abrasions on your hands.

Ajuga
(Also Called Bugle Plant)
Season: Blooms in May and June.
Description: Low-growing, six- to eight-inch-high mats of spreading green leaves with masses of dark-blue or deep-purple flowers.
Uses: Excellent as a ground cover for locations in light shade or sun, or in rock gardens.
Culture: Plant in spring or fall about six inches apart.
Light: Likes full sun or light shade.

Soil: Not fussy about soil; however, if bloom display diminishes after a few years, top dress with rich compost.

Propagation: Primarily by division.

Tips: Practically indestructible. A fine, colorful ground cover for shady areas.

Alyssum
(Also Called Basket of Gold)

Season: Blooms in early spring.

Description: Decorative, silver-gray foliage with a profusion of blooms in bright or lemon yellow. Plants grow twelve to fifteen inches high.

Uses: Use in rock gardens, in groups in perennial borders, or as edging plants. Also useful in baskets or patio containers.

Culture: Plant only in the spring.

Light: Likes sun although will bloom in light shade.

Soil: Any type of soil will do.

Propagation: Increase by division, cuttings, or seed.

Tips: One of the classic, early-spring perennials. This combines very well with many of the early-blooming bulbs.

Anchusa
(Also Called Perennial Forget-me-not)

Season: Blooms in May and June.

Description: Flowers resemble those of annual forget-me-nots. They are predominantly bright blue, but some varieties are white and purple. Foliage is robust and coarse, one to five feet tall.

Uses: Showy flowers look well in perennial borders.

Culture: Plant in spring only from six inches to two feet apart, depending on height of full-grown plant.

Light: Likes full sun.

Soil: Prefers deep, well-drained, not-too-heavy soil.

Propagation: By seed or division or cuttings.

Tips: Some varieties require staking. After bloom, foliage is apt to become unsightly. Overplant with annuals to cover the gap.

Anemone
(Also Called Windflower)

Season: Herbaceous types bloom in the fall.

Description: Slightly cup-shaped flowers in many colors, including white, pink, rose, and purple. Foliage is decorative, soft, and hairy.

Uses: Good in rock gardens, borders, and informally planted in woodlands.

Culture: Spring planting is best. Space nine to twelve inches apart.

Light: Likes partial shade.

Soil: Woodland soil is best, but well-drained ordinary garden soil will do.

Propagation: By division or cuttings.

Tips: In areas where winters are severe, protection is advised. (See Chapter 7 for other anemone varieties.)

Arabis
(Also Called Rock Cress)

Season: Blooms in spring.

Description: Blanket of white flowers on silvery foliage. Grows to a height of eight inches.

Uses: Excellent in rock gardens or on banks. Also can be used as edging or low-growing plant in perennial border.

Culture: Plant in spring from six to ten inches apart.

Light: Thrives in full sun or partial shade.

Soil: Prefers well-drained soil.

Propagation: Easily by seed or by division.

Tips: After blooming period, shear plant lightly to avoid scraggly appearance.

Aster
(Also Called Michaelmas Daisies)

Season: Blooms from June through late fall.

Description: Both three-foot-tall and dwarf varieties are covered with daisylike flowers ranging in color from white through lavender blue, pink, mauve, and violet.

Uses: Taller varieties are good in mixed borders. Dwarf varieties look well in rock gardens or as edging for perennial borders.

Culture: Plant in spring. Space some ten to eighteen inches apart, depending on the ultimate height of the variety.

Light: Likes full sun.

Soil: Any soil will do, but keep plants moist.

Propagation: Very similar to chrysanthemum culture. Each spring, dig the plant, divide, and replant the vigorous outside growth and divide the center.

Tips: Very popular in Europe and now becoming popular here. Should be used much more in this country.

Astilbe
(Also Called Spirea)
Season: Blooms in July.

Description: Flowers are borne in feathery panicles in shades of pink, red, and white. Foliage is dark green and fernlike. It remains attractive during the entire season, if not allowed to suffer from lack of moisture.

Uses: Excellent border plants. Can also be forced for use at Easter-time. Simply lift from ground in February, bring indoors, and place in sunny window.

Culture: Plant in spring or fall from ten to fifteen inches apart.

Light: Will grow in full sun but prefers partial shade.

Soil: Prefers a moist location but is not fussy about soil.

Propagation: Divide every three years.

Tips: A tough, very showy plant. Should be used much more in American gardens.

Balloon Flower
(Also Called Platycodon)
Season: Blooms from June until August.

Description: Showy, cup-shaped flowers are nearly three inches in diameter when wide open. Colors are purple-blue, white, and pink, both single and double varieties. Plants are erect and dense, reaching two to three feet in height. Mature specimens grow even taller.

Uses: Excellent border plants and long lasting cut flowers.

Culture: Plant in spring only from ten to fourteen inches apart.

Light: Likes full sun, but thrives in partial shade as well.

Soil: Prefers a moderately sandy loam with good drainage.

Propagation: By seed or by propagation. However, divide only in the spring before plants are established.

Tips: This is one of the latest perennials to show growth in the spring. Mark with a label to avoid damage when hoeing or weeding.

Balloon flower and astilbe grow beautifully together.

Bearded Iris
(Formerly Called German Iris)
Season: Blooms in May and June. Newer varieties often produce a second bloom in September. They are called rebloomers.

Description: Spectacular blooms in an incredibly wide range of color appear on stalks from two to five feet high. Foliage is a medium green, swordlike in appearance, and very handsome.

Uses: Use in borders. Dwarf varieties look well in rock gardens. Unsurpassed for cutting. Unsurpassed for accents. Unsurpassed!

Culture: Plant in fall from twelve to eighteen inches apart.

Light: Likes full sun but will grow in partial shade.

Soil: Prefers good garden loam.

Propagation: Dig and divide every three years. Discard old growth; cut and save only heavy rhizomes. Use a sharp knife and cut past borer holes and soft spots. Leave in sun for a day or dust with sulfur. Replant, making sure neck of tuber is just below the surface.

Tips: After blooming, cut stalks right down to rooty rhizome. When planting a group of the same variety, be sure that fans of leaves face outward with rhizomes facing inward in planting area. Sensational!

Bee Balm
(Also Called Monarda)
Season: Blooms in July and August.

Description: Red and lavender flowers along with many newer colors grow on tall, bushy, bold clumps.

Uses: Good for background planting, in herb gardens, or naturalized around ponds or along stream banks.

Culture: Plant in spring or fall about eighteen inches apart.

Light: Likes sun but will thrive in light shade.

Soil: Average soil will do.

Propagation: Divide every three years, preferably in the spring, and discard woody center portions.

Tips: Especially attractive to hummingbirds and bees. The leaves make a tea called Oswego tea. An old favorite, very hardy with brilliant flowers.

Bleeding Heart
(Also Called Dicentra)
Season: Blooms from May to July.

Description: Graceful, erect plants. Distinctly informal with oddly shaped flowers. Generally profuse in dainty racemes of rosy red or white hue.

Culture: Plant in spring or fall about two feet apart.

Uses: Ideal in perennial border or can be naturalized in woody areas.

Light: Likes partial shade.

Soil: Needs only a moderately rich, humus soil.

Propagation: By root cutting. Make cuttings of the fleshy, tuberous roots after blooming. Each cutting produces a new plant.

Tips: An old-fashioned favorite. Should be in everyone's garden.

Candytuft
(Also Called Iberis)
Season: Blooms in spring.

Description: Low-growing hedgy plant with dark-green foliage, which is evergreen in most

Columbine is one of late spring's most loved perennials.

areas. Covered with snow-white blossoms in May.

Uses: Excellent in rock gardens, as specimens in perennial borders, planted complementarily with spring bulbs. Can be trained as a low hedge.

Culture: Plant in spring or fall. Spreads, so plant a foot and a half apart and contain by pruning judiciously.

Light: Likes full sun but will bloom in light shade.

Soil: Prefers rich, well-drained garden soil.

Propagation: By seed, division, or cuttings.

Tips: Cut off dead tips after blooming, and plant will regain its rich-green color as new leaves form.

Chrysanthemum
Season: Blooms in fall.

Description: Grows in mound or shrublike form, is attractive during the summer before it blooms and is smothered with blossoms beginning in late August through fall. Single, double, pompon, spider, spoon, cushion, small, medium, and gigantic blooms. Color range includes everything except blue and true purple.

Uses: In borders, along walls, against evergreens, in rock gardens, and in beds. Superb, long-lasting cut flower.

Culture: Plant in spring from twelve to eighteen inches apart, depending on variety.

Light: Likes full sun.

Soil: Prefers quite fertile soil. Water generously throughout season.

Propagation: In spring, dig plants, divide, and plant vigorous side shoots. Discard center of plant.

Tips: For best results, flowers must be pinched. First pinch back main stem to two or three leaves after mum cutting or division is established. Growth appears above each leaf stem. Pinch back each break to two good leaves. Keep pinching until July 4.

Columbine
(Also Called Aquilegia)

Season: Blooms in May.

Description: Color range is extensive. Blooms are delicate, often bicolored, with long spurs. Foliage grows from one to four feet high. Flowers are borne on slender stalks.

Uses: Useful in borders, rock gardens, anywhere where garden is viewed closely. Lost when viewed from a distance.

Culture: Plant in spring about twelve inches apart.

Light: Grows in either full sun or partial shade.

Soil: Prefers a rich, well-drained, moist, slightly acidic soil.

Propagation: By seed, cuttings, or division. Crowns may lift over winter. To correct, simply dig and set back at proper level.

Tips: Seeds itself readily, but seedling may be ordinary.

Coreopsis
(Also Called Tickseed)

Season: Blooms in July.

Description: Daisy or starlike in appearance. The one-half- to 3-inch flowers are yellow, orange, maroon, red, and brownish purple. Plants grow from eight inches to four feet high. Wiry stems carry blooms.

Uses: Good as a border plant. Dwarf varieties are good in rock gardens.

Culture: Plant only in spring about fifteen inches apart.

Light: Likes full sun but will grow in partial shade.

Soil: Ordinary soil will do.

Propagation: From seed or divide in early spring or fall.

Tips: An old-fashioned favorite.

Day Lily
(Also Called Hemerocalis)

Season: Blooms in June and July.

Description: Plants grow from one and a half to five feet tall, forming a graceful mound of foliage. Flowers are conspicuous and lilylike, borne on stems that rise above foliage. Flowers come in a wide range of color. Plants are very versatile; some bloom in the day, some at night. Newer types have a decided fragrance, and the life of some individual flower species has been extended to several days.

Uses: In the perennial border, as accent plants, and in difficult situations (such as on slopes, banks, or around pools).

Culture: Set crown at soil level or slightly below. Spring planting is best or soon after blooming season. Young plants should be set two feet apart.

Light: Likes full sun or partial shade.

Soil: Not fussy about soil.

Propagation: Divide and replant every three or four years.

Tips: One of the most carefree and reliable flowers. No diseases. New varieties are stunning.

Hybrid day lilies are among the toughest of all flowers.

Delphinium

Season: Blooms in summer, with a second bloom in the fall.

Description: Large single or double blue, white, purple, and pink blooms arranged loosely on sprays from one to two feet high. The tall spires of flowers rise above foliage with a marked crown that spreads with age. Reaches to eight feet under ideal growing conditions.

Uses: Accents in perennial border, in specimens, or in groups by themselves.

Culture: Plant in spring about fifteen inches apart.

Light: Likes full sun but will tolerate light shade.

Soil: Very rich soil is essential, and it must be renewed each year.

Propagation: By division or by seed.

Tips: Not difficult to grow, but care is essential. Fertilize deeply. Cut spent flower stalks. Thin out weak shoots from established plants. Stake plants. Mulch with light material in winter. The fuss is worth every minute, since a well-grown delphinium is one of the most spectacular sights a gardener can achieve.

Dianthus
(Also Called Garden Pink)

Season: Most bloom in June.

Description: Flower stalks rise from a spreading mat of gray-green foliage. Flowers are fringed or toothed on the petals. Colors range from white and sulfur-yellow through shades of pink, mauve, red, and purple. Clovelike fragrance.

Uses: Use as low border plants in the perennial bed or in rock gardens. Useful as cut flowers.

Culture: Plant in spring from four to eighteen inches apart, depending on variety.

Light: Likes full sun.

Soil: Prefers warm, well-drained, nearly neutral soil.

Propagation: By seed, cuttings, or division.

Tips: Another old-fashioned flower that should be in every garden.

Evening primrose opens its yellow flowers late in the day.

Doronicum
(Also called Leopardsbane)

Season: Blooms in spring with tulips.

Description: Daisy flowers, simply formed but showy, grow on leafy plants.

Uses: Good cut flowers, useful in borders.

Culture: Plant in spring or fall about one foot apart.

Light: Does equally well in full sun or partial shade.

Soil: Prefers a moist soil.

Propagation: Divide every three years.

Tips: Foliage can become ragged by August. Overplant with annuals.

Evening Primrose
(Also Called Oenothera)

Season: Blooms in summer.

Description: Predominantly yellow flowers with four wide petals growing on stiffly upright plants about two feet high.

Uses: Good in groups in the mixed border or in rock gardens.

Culture: Plant in spring or fall about one foot apart.

Light: Likes full sun.

Soil: Average, well-drained soil will do.

Propagation: Divide every three years.

Tips: Extremely hardy and pest-free. A sure bet for the beginner.

Flax
(Also Called Linum)

Season: Blooms for a long time in summer.

Description: Five petaled blue flowers one-half to one and three-fourths inches in diameter borne on feathery clumps of slender flowering stalks from one to two feet high. Also in shades of red, yellow, and white.

Uses: Can be grown in rock gardens or toward the front of flower borders. Delicate but graceful and colorful.

Culture: Plant in spring only about one foot apart.

Light: Likes full sun.

Soil: Prefers well-drained soil.

Propagation: By division or cuttings. Plants divided in early spring often bloom the same year.

Tips: Heavy, waterlogged soil during winter will often kill flax (and other perennials).

Geum

Season: Blooms early, but moisture will keep it in bloom all summer.

Description: Forms leafy mounds, from which slender stalks up to two feet high bear single or clustered flowers of orange-red, yellow, or white.

Uses: Useful at the front of the perennial border and in rock gardens.

Culture: Plant in spring or fall about one foot apart.

Light: Likes full sun but thrives in partial shade.

Soil: Ordinary soil will do.

Propagation: Divide every two or three years. Can also be grown from seed.

Tips: One of the classic perennials. Easy to grow and pest-free. In short, a sure bet.

Gypsophila
(Also Called Perennial Baby's Breath)

Season: Blooms in June or July.

Description: Delicate, cloudlike flowers of white or pink grow on upright bushes to a height of four feet or so.

Uses: Useful in perennial borders and as cut flowers for trimming bouquets.

Culture: Plant in spring or fall from three to six feet apart, depending on variety.

Light: Likes full sun.

Soil: Prefers ordinary soil but lots of water.

Propagation: Does not divide well, since each plant has a long tap root. Buy plants from a nursery or grow from seed.

Tips: Flowers dry well. Work lime into the surface of the soil when planting and again each third year. When plant is fifteen to twenty inches high, place thin bamboo stakes closely around it, some six to eight per plant. After they are in place, cut off the top of the stakes. They should now be two feet above ground. Intertwine string into a tight corset to protect plant during wind and heavy rain.

Heuchera
(Also Called Coral Bells or Alumroot)

Season: Blooms from June on.

Description: Stout little plants with attractively shaped leaves carrying bell-shaped pink, red, or white flowers on long stems.

Uses: Excellent as edging for a border. Also good for cutting and in rock gardens.

Culture: Plant in spring or fall about one foot apart.

Light: Likes light shade or sun.

Soil: Any soil will do.

Propagation: Divide every third year.

Tips: Almost infallible. An old-fashioned favorite. Good for beginners.

Hosta
(Also Called Plaintain Lily or Funkia)

Season: Blooms in late summer.

Description: Primarily grown for its striking foliage and ability to grow in heavy shade. Handsome white and green variegated or solid-green foliage. Purple flowers on long stems.

Uses: As borders in shaded areas or as ground cover.

Culture: Plant in spring or fall about one foot apart.

Light: Likes deep shade.

Soil: Prefers moist, woody soil.

Propagation: Can be divided every few years.

Tips: Invaluable as plant for deep-shaded areas. An old-fashioned favorite with some interesting new varieties.

Japanese Iris

Season: Blooms from late June through July.

Description: Spectacular blooms, sometimes a full foot across. They are beardless and flat in form. Foliage is upright and stately, attractive throughout the season.

Uses: Showy in borders, along formal pool or streams. Stunning in cut flower arrangements.

Culture: Plant in spring or fall. Must have moisture, but water should not stand on it. Plant rhizomes two inches deep.

Light: Will grow in light shade but should have some sun every day.

Soil: Soil must be acidic. Lime is death to this variety.

Propagation: Divide in August or September when new plants are needed, after iris has reached considerable size. If at least three fans of leaves are retained for each division, they will probably bloom the following year.

Tips: Spectacular bloom. Must have plenty of moisture, but can survive drought after bloom since it goes into a rest period.

Lupine

Season: Blooms in June.

Description: Solid or bicolored flowers in shades of purple-blue and pink, as well as yellow, white, maroon, red, orange, and combinations. Foliage is green or gray-green, sometimes hairy. About three feet high.

Uses: Good in borders, in perennial beds, and for cutting.

Culture: Plant only in the spring about fifteen inches apart.

Light: Likes full sun.

Soil: Requires lots of moisture and rich soil.

Propagation: Taproot makes division difficult, but it can be done. Seed is preferable.

Tips: Must have protection from prevailing hot summer winds. Plant in bold groups.

Oriental Poppy

Season: Blooms in early summer.

Description: Very showy flowers on hairy silver-gray foliage. Colors include white, salmon, pink, crimson, red, and purple.

Uses: Useful as accents in borders and as cut flowers. But keep in mind that it is a showoff. Use restraint in planting.

Culture: Plant in fall about three feet apart. Place crown three inches below soil surface. Mulch the first winter to prevent heaving. Does not like to be transplanted, since it has a long taproot.

Light: Likes full sun but will thrive in half shade.

Soil: Prefers good garden loam, slightly moist with good drainage and some enrichment.

Propagation: By division every three or four years or by root cuttings three inches long. Be sure to place top of cutting nearest ground surface.

Tips: Foliage dies down after bloom. Interplant with annuals. When cutting, sear stems with flame and plunge into hot water for a minute before the usual soaking.

Peony

Season: Most bloom in June. However, some varieties bloom later in the season.

Hybrid peonies are all-time favorites for bouquet-making.

Description: Colors range from white through various shades of pink to deep red. There are also some yellows marked with shades of red and some pure sulfur yellows. Most are fragrant. Flowers are very large, growing on a shrublike plant averaging two and a half to three and a half feet high with spread equal to or exceeding the height.

Uses: Use in a perennial border, in front of shrubs, or as a flowering hedge. Excellent cut flowers.

Culture: Plant between September 1 and frost. Mulch during first winter to prevent heaving. Must be planted with the eye *exactly* one and a half inches below the surface of the soil.

Light: Likes full sun but will grow in partial shade.

Soil: When preparing soil, enrich with compost and rotted manure. Lightly feed annually after bloom. Not really finicky about soil but will do better if you follow above instructions.

Propagation: To increase stock, dig in the fall and divide (being sure to include three eyes). Plant one and a half inches below the surface.

Tips: Ants that crawl on the buds are harmless to the plant. Plants often live to be one hundred years old. New varieties are breathtakingly beautiful.

Phlox

Season: Blooms from summer to fall.

Description: Showy, fragrant florets in many colors on stems rarely exceeding two feet in height.

Uses: Invaluable in mixed borders. Good for cutting.

Culture: Plant in spring or fall from twelve to eighteen inches apart. Pinch out all but three or four stems in early spring. Roots cannot support more than this, and flowers will be stronger.

Light: Likes full sun but will grow in partial shade.

Soil: Prefers rich, moist soil.

Propagation: By division or by root cuttings.

Tips: Subject to mold growing on leaves during damp weather. To help combat this, leave plenty of room between plants for air circulation and do not plant near walls. Spraying with

Woods phlox (Phlox divaricata) *blooms in early spring; the color varies from lavender to blue. Needs part shade.*

Bordeaux Mixture or Captan helps. Many new varieties have been introduced from England within the last ten years.

Primrose
(Also Called Primula)
Season: Blooms in spring.

Description: Low-growing plants with single or clustered flowers in a wide range of colors including white, yellow, red, pink, magenta, purple, and blue.

Uses: Attractive in rock gardens, woodlands, and borders where it combines well with other spring-blooming plants. Can be bedded under dogwood, apple, or other high-branching trees as long as it has protection from summer sun.

Culture: Plant in spring only about one foot apart.

Light: Likes shade.

Soil: Prefers deep and well-enriched soil.

Propagation: By seed or division every third year.

Tips: An easy-to-grow favorite.

Shasta Daisy
Season: Blooms from June to August.

Description: White daisies, either single or double, with yellow centers blooming on sturdy upright plants with handsome foliage. Grows to three feet in height.

Uses: Good for cutting, borders.

Culture: Plant in spring about one foot apart.

Light: Likes full sun.

Soil: Prefers well-drained, moderately rich soil.

Propagation: Divide every other year to keep plants blooming. Also by seed.

Tips: An easy-to-grow favorite.

Tree Peonies
Season: Blooms in May.

Description: Shrubs with immense and beautiful flowers. Colors similar to those of herbaceous peonies. Handsome foliage. Can reach a height and spread of five feet.

Uses: Magnificent as accent plants in the border or as specimen shrubs. Cut flowers are spectacular.

Culture: In fall, dig a hole three feet wide by two feet deep in a well-drained location. Plant with the graft four inches below the surface. After deep frost, cover branches with one-bushel wooden basket weighted with a rock. After second year, work two ounces of Osmo-

Summer phlox hybrids are available in many colors.

Tree peony flowers are among the most coveted of all.

cote (14–14–14) into the top two inches of soil some twelve to fifteen inches around the branches. *Never cut back. Unlike peonies, branches do not die back.*

Light: Likes full sun but will grow in partial shade.

Soil: Prefers a neutral or just slightly alkaline soil. In areas where rainfall is heavy, prepare soil with just a bit of lime. Mix soil removed with damp peat, pure humus, or compost, as well as with one pound of bone meal.

Propagation: Cannot be propagated. Buy plants from nurseries.

Tips: Worth all of the trouble. One of the most beautiful flowers in existence.

Trollius
(Also Called Globeflower)
Season: Blooms in May and June, with sparser bloom throughout summer.

Description: Large, globular, or buttercup-like flowers in yellow bloom on attractive plant with dark-green leaves.

Uses: Good in perennial borders or in rock gardens.

Culture: Plant in spring or fall about one foot apart.

Light: Likes a shady location but will do well in sun as well.

Soil: Prefers rich soil with plenty of humus.

Propagation: By division or by seed. Divide every three years.

Tips: Ideal for adding a touch of bright yellow to a shady garden. Easy to grow. Highly satisfactory plant.

Veronica
(Also Called Speedwell)
Season: Blooms in midsummer.

Description: Spikes of lavender-blue, rose, or pink flowers rise from sturdy, spreading foliage.

Uses: Useful in rock gardens and perennial borders. One species, *Veronica filiformis,* may be used as a grass substitute in shaded areas. Taller varieties are good for cutting.

Culture: Plant in spring or fall.

Light: Likes sun.

Soil: Prefers well-drained soil enriched with compost or rotted manure.

Propagation: By seed or division. Should be divided every two years.

Tips: Foliage can become ragged, and some varieties tend to look weedy.

Canterbury bells (above), *pansies* (below left) *and English daisies* (below, right) *are all biennials.*

5
Biennials

Biennials are ignored to a great extent by many gardeners. Perhaps it is because they take two years from the seedling stage to the production of ripe seed. That is, you plant them in late spring of one year, and they flower and die the second year. However, they should not be overlooked, since they provide a spectacular display in the late spring, after the early spring bulb bloom has faded.

Sowing Biennial Seeds

First, prepare a seed bed as you would for annuals. After you have leveled the surface of the soil and have raked it until it is fine and powdering, use a sturdy stake or a hoe blade to make little furrows. These should be about nine inches apart and about one inch deep. Soak each row carefully with water. Use a watering can or a slow-running hose. Then sow the seeds, spacing them about one-half inch apart. Cover them gently with soil.

Taking Care of the Seedlings

When your seedlings have sprouted, begin to care for your biennials. Cultivate between rows and remove the weeds. When the seedlings have developed their second pair of leaves, transplant them into nursery beds out in the open. Or if you live in an area where winters are severe, prepare cold frames and plant them there. These beds should be prepared in the same way as the seedling beds, but mix some dried manure and bone meal into the soil. If you live in an area where summers are hot and dry, provide some shade for the seedlings. You can do this by placing lath frames over the beds. Be sure to keep your plants well watered during the dry spells of summer.

Planting Out of Biennials

If possible, select a cloudy day to transplant your biennials into their permanent positions. This should be done in September in areas where winters are mild (where temperatures rarely fall below ten degrees above zero) or in the spring (where winters are more severe). Dig up the plants with as big a soil ball as possible. You will find this task is made easier if you water your biennials the day before. Place the plants in flats and try not to disturb the ball of soil surrounding the plants. Dig good-sized holes and insert your plants. Pack the soil firmly around each plant. Then water the plants thoroughly with a sprinkler for about one-half hour. If the weather is very dry, water again in two or three days. If the weather is very sunny, provide some shade for the plants for a few days.

After the Bloom

During the second spring, water the plants whenever the ground is dry. Once they have bloomed, dig them up and put them on the compost heap. Most will not bloom again, and those that do won't bloom as well as newly started plants.

Protecting Your Biennials during the Winter

In areas where winter cold is severe, protection of biennials is recommended. Wait until after the ground is frozen to a depth of an inch or two. Then cover your plants with evergreen branches, salt hay, or marsh grass. Do not use leaves, since they tend to mat down and smother the plants. This protection prevents alternate freezing and thawing of the ground, causing heaving and exposing the roots.

In extremely cold areas, cold frames are recommended. However, be sure to provide ventilation when the temperature on the inside of the frame becomes hot. On very cold nights, cover the frame with mats, old rugs, or some other device. Snow on the cold frame is good protection.

List of Biennials

Bellis
(Also Called English Daisy)
Season: Blooms in spring.
Description: Low rosette plants that bear many single flower heads, each one to two inches in diameter. Grows on six-inch stalks. Colors include white, pink, and crimson.
Uses: Use in the spring border or as bed edging. Also good as underplanting for spring bulbs, such as tulips.
Culture: Sow in late May or June. Transplant to permanent positions in the fall or the following spring.
Light: Likes full sun.
Soil: Prefers moderately rich, well-drained, loamy soil.
Tips: Where winter temperatures dip below ten degrees above zero, winter over in a cold frame.

Canterbury Bells
(Also Called Campanula)
Season: Blooms in late spring and early summer.
Description: White, clear pink, or deep-purple flowers in single form, hose-in-hose, or cup and saucer form on bushy plants three or more feet high.
Uses: Good for bedding, in borders, or for cutting. Almost essential in any well-planned June garden.
Culture: Grow from seed planted in May, June, or July. Transplant seedlings before they become crowded. Should be grown under a lath for filtered sunshine. Set them in place in the fall or during the following spring in the place where they are to flower.
Light: Needs shade when young and full sun or partial shade when permanently planted.
Soil: Ordinary soil will do.
Tips: An old-fashioned favorite, and a spectacular one at that.

Forget-me-not
(Also Called Myosotis)
Season: Blooms in spring.
Description: Bedding plant that produces a dense carpet of small sky-blue, pink, or white flowers. Grows about nine inches high.
Uses: Good as underplanting in bulb garden or as a bedding plant in spring border.
Culture: Sow seeds in May or June. During hot summer, place a lath over the bed. Transplant in fall or early spring to permanent position from six to eight inches apart.

Light: Likes sun or light shade.

Soil: Prefers slightly acidic soil, rich with humus.

Tips: Often reseeds itself.

Foxglove
(Also Called Digitalis)

Season: Blooms in June. Often has a second bloom in late August and September.

Description: Closely spaced, thimble-shaped flowers that hang daintily downward in a spirelike effect. Colors are rose, white, yellow, and purple. Spikes rise two to four feet over generous, handsome, leafy bases.

Uses: Good for border background, naturalizing, and cutting.

Culture: Sow in late May or June. Transplant to permanent positions in the fall or the following spring.

Light: Likes sun or light shade.

Soil: Prefers medium, well-drained soil.

Tips: Leaves are poisonous if eaten. However, they are used as a base for important heart-disease medicines. Often reseeds itself.

Iceland Poppy

Season: Blooms in April.

Description: Flower stems are one foot high, with flowers ranging from white through yellow and orange. Crimson variety is called Red Cardinal.

Uses: Excellent for cutting and for bedding.

Culture: Sow seed where plant is to flower, since it does not like to be transplanted. May or June is the time to sow. Blooms the following spring. Thin to four inches as soon as plant is big enough to handle and later to six to nine inches apart.

Light: Sun or partial shade will do.

Soil: Prefers well-drained average soil.

Tips: Often reseeds itself. Alpine variety good for rock gardens.

Pansy

Season: Blooms in May, June, and July, and if blossoms are cut after blooming, flowers until frost.

Description: Blue, purple, red, yellow, white, and copper flowers growing to one foot high on bushy foliage.

Uses: Good as underbedding for bulbs or as border edging.

Culture: Can be grown from seed. However, it is far more satisfactory to buy flats in the spring from the nursery.

Light: Full sun or medium shade will do.

Soil: Prefers well-drained, ordinary soil.

Tips: If allowed to go to seed in midsummer, will reseed, but seed often not true to parent.

Sweet William
(Also Called Dianthus Barbatus)

Season: Blooms in June.

Description: Many varieties have white central eyes surrounded by bands of other colors, primarily in the red color range. Foliage is compact and handsome. Clove fragrance. Grows from one to two feet tall.

Uses: Good for beds, as underplanting for bulbs, and for cutting.

Culture: Sow seed in May or June. Transplant to permanent position in the fall or during the following spring. Plant some ten inches apart.

Light: Grows in sun or partial shade.

Soil: Not fussy about soil.

Tips: Often reseeds itself. However, new plants are often mongrel and do not resemble parent plant. In milder climates, will winter over and bloom several seasons. Treat as perennial in this case.

Wallflower
(Also Called Cheiranthus)

Season: Blooms in May and June.

Description: Bushy plants that grow up to two feet tall with spikes of velvety flowers. Colors are red and yellow.

Uses: Generally grown as bedding plants for spring garden.

Culture: Plant in May or June and transplant to permanent position in the fall or during the following spring.

Light: Grow in partial shade or full sun.

Soil: Prefers well-drained soil.

Tips: It is recommended that you transplant young plants twice during their early growth. This encourages root growth. Also, pinch back the tops of the plant once or twice to ensure a bushy plant. Set out ten to twelve inches apart.

Miniature roses are great to grow in the ground or in pots. This one, called Twinkles, is shown actual size.

6
Roses

Who can resist a perfect rose? And in fact, with the proper preparation anyone can grow beautiful roses—and grow them just about anywhere. There are varieties suited to all tastes and all climates. The varieties discussed in this chapter, however, are generally adaptable to all parts of the United States. If you live in a region where many plants simply do not thrive, check with your local nursery, a botanical garden, or the department of horticulture at your state university for varieties suitable for your area. Other than that, for just a few dollars and a little time and energy, your reward will be blooms of what many consider the most beautiful flower in existence.

Where to Plan Your Rose Garden

Roses need at least five or six hours of unfiltered sunlight a day in order to grow successfully. The best location is one with sunshine from early in the morning until late in the afternoon. However, if your plot of ground does not offer this much sunlight, don't hesitate to plant roses anyway. Many gardeners grow them successfully on the east or west sides of their houses, where they receive sun for only half of the day. If some shade is inevitable, keep in mind that the morning sun is better for roses than the afternoon sun. This is because the sun burns the dew off of the roses in the morning, allowing leaf diseases less chance to develop.

Do not put other plants in your rose garden. Roses must be tended carefully and in different ways from most other plants. They resent other plants, bushes, or trees competing for moisture and nourishment. And besides, they look better off by themselves.

When you plan your bed, make sure that you have access to the bases of all plants. This will make chores such as watering, fertilizing, pruning, and removing dead blooms easier for you. If there is access only from one side, make the bed between eighteen and twenty-four inches wide. If there is access from both sides, the bed can be about one yard wide.

When you plan your rose bed, be sure to check the ultimate growing heights of the bushes. Place the tall bushes in the rear and the lower ones in the front.

Generally speaking, roses should be placed in formal beds (that is, in planned geometric forms). They lend themselves beautifully to this treatment.

The Different Kinds of Roses

Most people who are starting out with rose gardening think that all roses produce single blooms on long stems, like those available at the local florist. However, there are many kinds of roses.

The Hybrid Teas
Hybrid teas are the everblooming roses, called monthly roses in some areas, and are the most widely grown of all types of roses. They are highly desirable, with flowers resembling those you buy at the florist. Generally, they are on long stems and are excellent for cutting. The buds are delicately formed, the fragrances are lovely, and the fully opened flowers are very beautiful. They range in height from two feet to six feet, and they are available in a wide range of colors.

Floribunda Roses
The flowers on these bushes grow in clusters and have shorter stems than hybrid teas. If you want a mass of color rather than a cutting garden, floribundas are your best bet. They are very hardy and grow everywhere in the United States. The varieties and colors are extensive.

Grandiflora Roses
Grandiflora roses have characteristics of both hybrid teas and floribunda roses, being a cross between the two varieties. The flowers usually appear in clusters; however, there are often long-stemmed flowers comparable to hybrid teas. They are usually large, so space them further apart than you would hybrid teas. Some grow to well over six feet, and many have a diameter of three feet or more. Since these roses have been introduced fairly recently, a large variety of types, such as those found in hybrid teas, is not yet available; however, each year more and more types make their bow. They are quite beautiful and well worth your investigation.

Tree Roses
Tree roses are grafted onto special rootstock. The stock produces a trunk from three to five feet high. Above the stock, all of the previously described types of roses can be grafted. In fact, even miniature roses are sometimes grafted on root stock. Variety is limited and they are costly, because much is involved in producing them. But if you want a real conversation piece, plant a tree rose. They need special protection in the winter.

Climbing Roses
Canes of climbers grow anywhere from eight feet long to twenty feet or more. They cannot stand alone, and they need support in the form of a fence or trellis to keep them from crawling along the ground. There are some varieties (the rambler, for instance) that bloom only once a year. Others have been bred from hybrid teas and floribundas; these bloom in late spring, as well as during the summer and in the fall. These are called "everblooming," while those that bloom only in June and again in the fall are called "repeat blooming."

Miniature Roses
Miniature roses are beautiful little jewels that grow only about eight inches high. They are raised exactly the same way as other roses. There is a wide variety of colors and types available, including climbers that grow only three to five feet tall and tree roses that grow only about ten inches tall.

Other Roses
Old-fashioned roses are available at some specialty nurseries, but generally they are hard to find. Most bloom in June without a repeat bloom. Recently, there has been an upsurge of interest in these rather quaint specimens.

The Best Values in Roses

Rule number one when it comes to growing roses is: Don't buy bargain roses. Oh yes, plants that sell for eighty-nine cents in the supermarkets may perform reasonably after a few years, but why bother with them? Good, sturdy, vigorous rose bushes are available through the better mail-order houses or through your local nursery at slightly higher costs. And considering the years and years of joy they will bring you, they are worth every extra cent.

Planting Roses

If you buy roses through the mail, you probably will receive bare root plants; that is, there will be no soil around the roots and the plants will be packaged in a plastic bag. The rose growers will mail them to you at the proper time for your area. If you buy from the local nursery, the plants may be bare rooted, or they may be planted in tubs. Plant them after danger of frost has passed.

Newly arrived roses can stay in their shipping carton for several days, but be sure to place them in a cool place. If you must delay planting a week or ten days, then heel in the roses. To do this, dig a trench, place the plants in the trench, and cover them completely (roots and stems) with dirt. If they arrive wrapped in plastic, foil, or kraft paper, just bury the entire package until you are ready for planting.

The night before you are ready to plant, take the roses out of their wrappings or dig them up out of your trench and soak the roots in a pail of water for twelve to eighteen hours. Place them in an unheated garage or a cool sheltered area. Do not place them outdoors where the sun or wind can get at them, since these elements tend to dry out the canes.

Dig a hole eighteen inches deep and eighteen inches wide. That is a big hole, but your reward in bloom and vigorous plants more than compensates for the work involved. If your soil is hard clay or does not drain well, dig even deeper—say another two or three inches. Where drainage is poor, place a layer of stones, broken flower pots, or broken bricks in the bottom of the hole. You can also use sand. The roots of your roses need air and will not thrive in a soil that is constantly wet.

Mix a half-inch layer of bone meal in with some soil at the bottom of the hole. Nourishment will be released slowly to the roots of your plants. Once you have done this, fill the hole

Hybrid tea roses give fragrant bloom from June on.

with water to ascertain whether or not the soil drains well. This also thoroughly wets the surrounding soil so that when you plant your rose and water it the moisture will go to the roots. Check your rose bush. If there are broken roots or canes, prune them off. Any long roots can also be cut off to assure that your plant fits in the hole.

Now mix the pile of soil you have dug out with a half cupful of complete fertilizer. Rose food, or 5-10-5 will do. Dehydrated cow manure is also good for the plant; use two or three full coffee cans of the manure. Add compost or peat moss to your soil.

Now that you have taken care of the preliminaries, it is time to plant your roses. Cut back all rose canes (regardless of variety) to two or three buds or shoots on each stem. The roots will support this growth vigorously. Next build a cone of soil in the hole you have dug. Spread the roots over the cone before you fill the hole with soil. Be sure that you plant your rose at the proper depth. If you look at the bottom part of the stem, you will notice a swollen area. This is where the plant was grafted. This graft should be just above the level of the soil. If you plant too deeply, your rose will probably not sprout new cane growth in future years. If you plant too shallowly, winter damage may occur to the graft.

Hold the plant in its proper place and fill the hole about two-thirds full with soil. Pack it down lightly as you fill. Water the hole with a gentle stream of water and let it soak in. You do this to be sure that the soil will fill in between the roots and to be sure that the roots have sufficient moisture. Once the water has soaked in, fill the hole completely with your soil and mound it up around the canes to a height of about eight or ten inches above ground. Leave this mound of soil on for about a week, since it will protect the canes from the elements until the root system has established itself.

You may wish to protect your bush with burlap or a plastic bag. If you use plastic, be sure to provide a number of holes for air and ventilation. Otherwise, your plant may die.

Planting Distances

Areas where the winters are very severe require closer planting than that recommended below.

Hybrid Teas. Plant these at least eighteen inches to two feet apart. Where it is very mild, plant them three feet apart.

Floribundas. Depending on variety, plant from fourteen to twenty-four inches apart.

Grandifloras. Plant spreading varieties at least three feet apart. Plant others two and one-half feet apart.

Climbers. Plant from eight to sixteen feet apart.

Miniatures. Plant anywhere from a few inches to one foot apart.

Watering Roses

Roses need a great deal of water in order to grow and bloom properly. It is far better to soak the ground thoroughly (to a depth of twelve inches) once a week than to lightly sprinkle it two or three times a week. Keep in mind that usually, especially during the hot summer months, rainfall will not provide enough water.

You must help nature out and provide the extra water.

There are several different ways to water your plants. Most people simply take the nozzle off the hose and let the water slowly dribble around the base of the plant. If you use this system, you run the risk of excessive runoff, and the water may wash soil away from surface roots. A soaker hose, which may be purchased from your nursery or hardware store, is a far better method of watering. Or you can purchase a water wand, which enables you to direct the flow of water. Sprinkler hoses turned upside down will also do the trick.

Fertilizing Roses

Another necessary facet of the care of roses is fertilization. In order to have beautiful roses, you must feed them. They are voracious eaters, needing nitrogen, phosphorus, and potassium in large amounts. Generally, there is not enough of these elements in the soil. The widely available all-purpose fertilizers will do the trick for you. Either 5–10–5, 6–10–4 or 4–6–4, etc., will do. Special rose foods are also available that provide all the elements needed for good growth.

The first time you apply the fertilizer is in the spring, when new growth is well underway and danger of severe frost has passed. Apply it a second time near the end of June, and apply it a third time near the middle of August where it is cold in the winter or near mid-September where it is warm. Apply fertilizers around the base of the plant. A quarter of a cup usually suffices for small- and medium-sized roses, but a half cup is suitable for larger plants. After you feed the plant, soak it thoroughly with water. Roses prefer neutral to slightly acidic soil. If your soil is heavily alkaline, consult your local nursery about acidic additives.

Mulching Roses

Mulching is another important aspect of the care of roses. By mulching, you prevent the ground from drying out during the hot, dry months of summer. Mulch also serves to keep

Goldilocks floribunda rose is outstanding for garden use.

weeds down, and if attractive, can enhance the appearance of your bed of roses.

Many good mulching materials are sold; however, you can also use grass clippings (readily available at no cost to you), decomposed compost, or even pebbles or small stones. Organic materials, however, have the advantage of decomposing and enriching the soil. Mulch from one-half to two inches deep, depending on the material you use. Your local nursery can advise you about this.

Pruning Roses

If you want your roses to be healthy and vigorous and to bloom prolifically, cut back or prune them twice a year. The first pruning is done in the beginning of November or shortly after the autumn leaves fall. Start the second pruning in the middle of March.

The November operation is a simple one, the main purpose being to remove some of the very tall growth. The winter winds tend to whip around the taller canes and loosen the roots, so prune back one-quarter to one-third from the top. Cut back all canes and most of the side branches also.

The March operation should be started when buds begin to show on the canes. Through the winter a rose bush becomes misshapen with dead wood and too many small twigs. It may well look like a briar patch. So in order to make way for the new growth, you must prune.

In the spring, cut off all dead, broken, or diseased wood. In addition, cut away any old stumps that were not cut away in prior years. In this case, cut as close as possible to the crown of the bush. Leave the smallest possible stub. In addition, any canes that are several years old should also be cut away. They lack the vigor of new growth, and by removing them you make way for new canes.

Usually, the wood of the rose is hard and difficult to cut. The most satisfactory way to remove the old wood is with lopping shears, which are available at your nursery or hardware store. Canes that have been winter killed should be cut back. You can spot them easily because they are black instead of a healthy green. Also look for cankers, which are fungous growths that attack roses during the winter. These are brownish in color with deep burgundy edges. Ultimately they will spread, encircle the cane, and kill it. They should be removed as soon as they are visible. Again, cut back to healthy green wood.

There are two schools of thought among rose experts about pruning. Some advocate high pruning, while others choose low. Those who choose high pruning cut back to twenty-four inches. Lower-growing roses are not pruned until they reach that height. Low pruners cut to from eight to ten inches. The high pruners feel that they get more bloom, albeit smaller flowers. The low pruners claim their roses are larger and more beautiful. In addition, low pruners force low-growing foliage. Aesthetically, their roses may well be more attractive, having a bushier appearance.

There are also those who advocate a middle ground. They cut grandifloras to around two feet, hybrid teas to one and a half feet, and floribundas to one foot. In warmer areas the height will range from eighteen to thirty inches after pruning.

Once you have removed the old wood, cut the canes to the height you want. Make the cuts with sharp pruning shears and cut at a forty-five-degree angle about a half inch above a well-developed bud that faces out. This helps keep the center of the bush open both to the air and to the sun. If you cut straight across or if you cut higher than one-half inch, you risk trouble from disease. If you cut closer you will probably kill the bud, since it will dry out. Should you prune before the buds are developed in the spring, you may have to shorten some of the canes later in order to leave the recommended half-inch length.

Sometimes a cane sprouts double or triple buds and each of them grows. Since the nourishment which supplies one cane is divided between two or three canes, the results are disappointing. Prune below such growth or

Hybrid tea rose Dixie Belle is deliciously scented.

Hybrid tea rose Mexicana has vivid orange flowers.

remove one or two buds from the cane with your fingers so that only one bud develops into a cane.

Sometimes when cuts are made too far above a bud, a "hatrack" effect develops. Eventually, the bud dies and renders the bush more susceptible to disease. When this situation occurs, cut below the "hatrack," removing part of the healthy cane as well.

If you have pruned properly, your rose bush will look rather sad; however, it is in better shape than one less pruned. In a few short weeks, vigorous new growth will sprout. Keep in mind that the roots are still intact and that they pour the nourishment into the plant.

After you have made all of your cuts, there is one more thing to do. All ends which are half an inch or more in diameter must be protected. This keeps moisture out, discourages diseases, and prevents insects from eating at the soft core of the cane. Simply paint each end with shellac, tree-wound paint, Elmer's Glue, asphalt paint, or any waterproof material.

Protecting Roses Through the Winter

In most parts of the United States, roses are hardy and survive reasonably hard winter weather. If you live in an area where tempera-

tures rarely fall below zero, little winter protection is necessary for roses that are established. The primary damage will be the breaking of canes by the wind, and fall pruning will spare you this difficulty. As an added precaution, you can tie the canes together with some twine.

In areas where winter temperatures drop below zero with frequency, provide winter protection for your roses. The most effective way is to mound up the soil around the base of the bush to a height of eight to ten inches. Bring the soil from another part of the garden, for if you scrape it from the bed around the roses you will probably expose the roots to cold damage. If you live in an area where temperatures fall lower than zero consistently, add several inches of hay or straw mulch to the mound. Check with your local nursery as to whether or not this additional protection is necessary.

Special consideration should be given to tree roses in areas where the weather is extreme. Cut the roots on one side, bend the tree over carefully, and cover the entire tree with a few inches of dirt. Climbers can be protected by laying the canes on the ground, lightly binding them with twine, and covering them with soil in the same way. After danger of severe cold has passed, generally late March to early April in most places, carefully remove the soil by hand. Avoid damaging new bud growth.

Floribunda roses like Castanet produce bouquets of bloom to enjoy in the garden, or to cut for indoors.

Daffodils are an outstanding example of flowers that grow from hardy bulbs planted in fall for spring bloom.

7
Hardy Bulbs

The backbone of the spring garden is the hardy bulb. And what glorious displays of color they provide. Beginning with the snowdrops, winter aconite, and *Iris reticulata;* continuing with crocus, then hyacinths and daffodils; and finally ending with the riotous blaze of color provided by the tulips, they are irresistible. Bulbs are extremely versatile, taking their place in formal beds, in borders, in rock gardens, in sun and shade, or naturalized in meadows and woodlands.

Most gardeners plant crocuses, daffodils, hyacinths, and tulips, and they ignore many of the "minor" bulbs, bulbs that produce some of the most beautiful flowers to be grown. In this chapter, you will read about many of the less-known bulbs. Experiment with them. Be adventurous! You have nothing to lose and everything to gain. Your reward will be great as you watch the ones you have selected sprout through the ground, grow, and finally bloom.

Planting Bulbs

Most of the bulbs available in this country like a good, well-drained soil. If your soil is not good, add compost, well-rotted manure, peat moss, or other organic material to the soil when you plant your bulbs. Incidentally, never use fresh manure when you plant your bulbs. It would burn the tender roots as they sprouted.

Bulbs thrive in most soils. However, if drainage conditions are not up to par, they rot. If there is an area in your garden which is waterlogged most of the time, plant your bulbs elsewhere. This is not to say that bulbs do not need moisture, in fact, they need a lot of moisture. But if they sit in soggy soil, they will not thrive.

Fertilizing Bulbs

Until recently, bone meal was considered the best fertilizer to use when planting bulbs. Recently, in Holland, bulb breeders have been experimenting with different kinds of fertilizers. Sewage sludge has emerged as a miracle fertilizer for bulbs. This is available in this country under the brand name of

Milorganite, and it is recommended highly for anyone interested in raising spectacular flowers from bulbs. Simply place a tablespoon of it in the bottom of the hole for your bulb. Mix it into the soil and then watch the results the following spring. You can also add a teaspoonful of bone meal, the traditional food for bulbs. It will do no harm.

Each fall, sprinkle more Milorganite on the surface of the soil where your bulbs are planted. Do this every year, since bulbs need to be fed in order to bloom their best.

Plant all hardy bulbs in the fall, using a bulb planter (a tool especially designed for digging holes for bulbs) or simply a trowel. When you dig the hole, flatten it out on the bottom so that the bulb sits on soil and not on air. Pour in your bone meal and/or Milorganite, mix it with the soil, place the bulb in the hole, and cover it with dirt. Then *water it!* That's all there is to it.

If you are planting a bed of bulbs, it's probably more satisfactory to dig up the entire area you wish to plant, fertilize it, then place the bulbs where you want them.

Another way to plant bulbs is to naturalize them. Some bulbs particularly lend themselves to this treatment. They include allium, chionodoxa, colchicum, crocus, eranthis, fritillaria, galanthus, leucojum, lily, grape hyacinth, and daffodil or jonquil. To do this, simply toss a handful of bulbs on the ground and plant them where they land. This method is especially effective in woodlands, meadows, or in areas where the grass is not mowed. Do not plant in this manner if you have to mow the grass during the spring. If you do, you will mow the ripening foliage of the bulbs and ultimately kill them.

If conditions are satisfactory, most bulbs multiply. Little bloom indicates crowded conditions. Watch the blooming, and if you find that the spring show is not quite up to par, dig up the bulbs, separate them, and replant them. Do this when the leaves have died down or when the leaves have turned half yellow.

When you plant your bulbs in a bed or border, keep in mind that the foliage must be allowed to ripen before cutting. Either plan for this by overplanting a reasonably tall-growing plant, which will cover the withering foliage, or by binding the foliage into tidy bunches with twine. This is because the leaves manufacture the food, which is returned to the bulb for storage after the leaves fade. They must have this food in order to bloom satisfactorily the following year. Some people ignore this and strangely enough, do have reasonable bloom. But for the most satisfactory growth, don't cut the leaves.

Do not plant single bulbs. A single flower will look lost in your garden. Plant them in groups of at least five or six. Don't mix too many colors together. This is particularly true for tulips. It is better to mix two or, at the most, three different varieties of tulips in a location than to mix a rainbow of varieties. If you use three varieties, make one of them white. Generally speaking, don't plant bulbs in a straight line, for they look ridiculous when they bloom.

After your bulbs have bloomed, cut the flower heads off. This is because you do not want the strength of the plant to go into producing seeds, instead of returning to the bulb.

List of Hardy Bulbs

A selection of bulbs generally available in the United States follows.

Allium Albopilosum

Season: Blooms in June.

Description: A big ball of star-shaped lilac flowers on sturdy two-foot-high stems.

Uses: Good for cutting.

Culture: Plant in fall five inches deep and nine inches apart.

Light: Likes light shade or sun.

Soil: Well-drained ordinary soil will do.

Propagation: Lift and divide every three or four years.

Tips: Very long-lasting in the garden or as a cut flower. Soak overnight in cold water to remove onion smell.

Allium Beesianum

Season: Blooms in June.

Description: Six- to twelve-inch-high plants with blue flowers similar to allium moly.

Uses: As cut flowers or in the rock garden.

Be sure to plant plenty of daffodils to cut and enjoy indoors in natural arrangements like this one.

Culture: Plant in fall, three inches deep and six inches apart.

Light: Semishade to full sun will do.

Soil: Ordinary soil, however, prefers more moisture than other alliums.

Propagation: Lift and divide every three or four years.

Tips: Nice cut flower. Soak overnight in cold water to remove onion smell.

Allium Giganteum

Season: Blooms in July.

Description: Immense, bright lilac-colored flowers which grow from four to five feet high. Flowers start green, turn to lilac, and as they mature, turn green again.

Uses: In backgrounds of beds and borders, as novelty specimens, and especially as cuttings.

Culture: Plant in fall, four inches deep and one foot apart.

Light: Any light except deep shade will do.

Soil: Well-drained soil that is not too rich.

Propagation: Lift and divide every four years.

Tips: Leaves smell like onions if bruised; however, soaking them overnight in cold water kills the smell. Blooms last for three weeks when cut. Be sure to stake them.

Allium Moly
(Also Called Lily Leek or Golden Garlic)

Season: Blooms in June.

Description: Golden-yellow blooms on onion-like foliage. Grows about one foot high.

Uses: Good in rock gardens or in perennial beds.

Culture: Plant in fall, three inches deep and six inches apart.

Light: Will thrive in light shade as well as sun.

Soil: Well-drained ordinary soil will do.

Propagation: Lift and divide every three or four years.

Tips: Very hardy, good for naturalizing and for cutting. Onion smell can be removed by soaking cut flowers overnight in cold water.

Anemone
(Also Called Windflower)

Season: Blooms in March and early April.

Description: Daisy-type flowers in blue, pink, white, scarlet, and mixed colors, depending on variety. Grows from six to nine inches tall with compact foliage.

Uses: Good in rock gardens or in beds.

Culture: Plant in fall, six to twelve bulbs in a clump some two inches deep. Plant less-hardy varieties in spring.

Light: Likes light shade.

Soil: Prefers moist, well-drained, good soil.

Tips: Hardiness varies. If you live in a cold area, plant these in the spring, dig them in the fall, and store over winter.

Varieties: Blanda Blue Star, Pink Star, Radar, White Splendor, DeCaen, Fulgens, St. Brigid.

Camassia
(Also Called Quamash or Camass)

Season: Blooms in May or June.

Description: Star-shaped flowers of light blue, white, or purplish blue, growing one and a half feet to three feet high.

Uses: Good in borders or beds.

Culture: Plant in early fall, four to five inches deep and six to eight inches apart.

Light: Full sun to light shade will do.

Soil: Most any soil will do, including heavy clay if it isn't waterlogged. Keep moist.

Tips: Fertilize every year or plant will wane.

Chionodoxa
(Also Called Glory-of-the-snow)

Season: Blooms in March.

Description: Star-shaped, light- or clear-blue flowers with white eyes that face the sun. Grows six to seven inches high. Little flower spikes hold about twelve to fifteen flowers each.

Uses: Good in rock gardens or naturalized.

Culture: Plant in fall, three inches deep and three inches apart.

Light: Likes sun or partial shade.

Soil: Prefers a sandy soil but will thrive in ordinary soil.

Propagation: Multiplies readily. Dig every three or four years and divide to increase stock.

Tips: Very delicate little flower, a pleasant sight during the cold days of March.

Colchicum
(Also Called Autumn Crocus or Meadow Saffron)

Season: Blooms in October.

Description: Crocus-type flowers that bloom before foliage appears. Runty foliage disappears soon after it appears in spring.

Uses: Good for naturalizing or in rock gardens.

Culture: Plant in August with tops of bulbs two to three inches beneath surface. Do not transplant as long as plants continue to bloom satisfactorily.

Light: Likes partial shade or sun.

Soil: Deep, porous soil enriched with leaf mold or compost is ideal. Keep reasonably moist. When in foliage, should never be allowed to dry out.

Tips: An interesting novelty for fall rock gardens.

Crocus
(Hybrids and Species)

Season: Blooms in February and March. Species varieties tend to bloom earlier than hybrid varieties.

Description: Large-flowered bulb that blooms in white, blue, purple, yellow and combinations.

Uses: As a harbinger of spring, for color during the dreary late-winter days.

Culture: Plant in fall, two to three inches deep and three inches apart. Mix a tablespoon

Pickwick crocus has white flowers feathered with purple.

of Milorganite or bone meal in the hole before planting.

Light: Likes full sun.

Soil: Prefers well-drained soil.

Propagation: Multiplies readily. Lift and divide every three or four years.

Tips: Even if you only plant a few, they will give you a lift toward the end of winter.

Varieties: Hybrids, called Dutch crocus, are the large ones. Little Dorrit is light blue with a silver cast; Peter Pan is pure white; Pickwick is silver-lilac; Yellow Mammoth is yellow; *Purpurea grandiflora* is deep purple.

Species are slightly smaller than hybrids but bloom earlier. Blue Bird is blue with a white margin; Blue Peter is deep purple with a golden throat; Goldilocks is yellow; Gypsy Girl is butter gold with chocolate brown; Lady Killer is deep purple and white; Ruby Giant is burgundy; Purity is white.

Dutch Iris

Season: Blooms in May.

Description: Delicate irislike flowers on eighteen-inch stems in purples, yellows, whites, blues, and combinations. Seen often at the florist.

Uses: Beautiful for cutting or for spots of formal color in borders.

Culture: Plant in fall some four inches deep and six inches apart. Fertilize soil with bone meal or Milorganite.

Light: Likes full sun.

Soil: Prefers sandy, well-drained soil.

Propagation: Multiplies readily. Dig every third year and replant.

Tips: Spanish and English Iris are similar but bloom in June.

Eranthis
(Also Called Winter Aconite)

Season: Blooms in February.

Description: Small, low-growing foliage with yellow-buttercup flowers.

Uses: A harbinger of spring.

Culture: Plant tubers in late summer. Mix bone meal or Milorganite in the ground. Plant two inches deep and about three or four inches apart.

Light: Light shade or sun will do.

Soil: Requires good garden soil.

Propagation: Seeds freely if left undisturbed.

Tips: Flourishes in the shade. Good for woodland banks where, once established, it multiplies readily. Leave undisturbed and bloom will continue for a lifetime. The earliest of all spring bulbs.

Fritillaria Imperialis
(Also Called Snake-head Lily)

Season: Blooms in April.

Description: Two- to three-foot-high spikes in orange, yellow, and red bell-like flowers.

Uses: Accent plants in spring borders. Not for cutting, since odor is not particularly pleasant.

Culture: Plant in fall, three to four inches deep and six to eight inches apart. In colder areas, mulch in the fall with compost or rotted manure.

Light: Likes full sun or light shade.

Soil: Prefers good, well-drained soil. Keep well watered during hot summer months.

Propagation: Lift and divide every three or four years.

Tips: Can be capricious and difficult to grow, but if it likes its location, will thrive. Hardiness is touchy in colder areas.

Galanthus
(Also Called Snowdrop)

Season: Blooms in February.

Description: Small, white flowers with markings. Foliage disappears shortly after bloom.

Uses: A harbinger of spring.

Culture: Plant bulbs as soon as they arrive. Most nurseries do not stock galanthus in August, which is the best time to plant them. Order them through one of the better bulb houses. Plant three inches deep and three inches apart.

Light: Does best in shade under bushes, under trees, or along wooded paths.

Soil: Likes rich, woodsy, well drained soil.

Propagation: Multiplies readily. It is not necessary to lift and divide; however, do so to increase your stock.

Tips: A welcome sight in the spring. Plant a lot for a good show. In sheltered spots, even blooms in January.

Hyacinth

Season: Blooms in April.

Description: Flamboyant clusters of pink, red, white, blue, purple, yellow, and orange flowers on tall stalks. Highly fragrant. One of the most popular of the bulbs. Grows to one foot tall.

Uses: Good for formal beds, or if properly planned, in informal settings.

Culture: Plant in fall. Put a tablespoon of bone meal or Milorganite in the hole before planting.

Light: Thrives in partial shade or full sun.

Soil: Prefers well-drained, rich soil.

Propagation: Some varieties, like Orange Boven, multiply readily. Others do not.

Tips: Generally, sensational the first year, and as the years pass becomes less so, throwing up single spikes with fewer flowers. Much more adaptable to informal beds after being in the ground a few years. Some people buy new ones each year and plant the old ones in cutting gardens or informal settings. Beautiful and reasonable in price.

Iris Reticulata

Season: Blooms in very early spring. Often mid-February.

Description: Miniature iris in purples, blues, and yellows growing from four to nine inches high. Foliage withers after bloom.

Uses: Almost the first flower to bloom in spring. Put close by where you can see it. Will even pop up through snow.

Culture: Plant in fall, three inches deep and three inches apart.

Light: Partial shade or full sun will do.

Soil: Slightly rich soil is best.

Propagation: Multiplies but leave flowers where they are for the best results.

Tips: One of the very fragrant flowers of spring. Inexpensive, easy to grow, and should be planted by everyone.

Leucojum
(Also Called Snowflakes)

Season: Blooms in March and April.

Description: Foot and a half-high stalks bear four or more white bells. An autumn variety bears flowers on four-inch stems. Another has six-inch stems.

Uses: Use in rock gardens and borders, or as a harbinger of spring.

Culture: Plant in late summer or early fall, two to three inches deep and three to four inches apart. Autumn varieties should be planted one to two inches apart.

Light: Will thrive in partial shade.

Soil: Prefers well-drained soil.

Propagation: For best results, plant and leave alone. Multiplies, but don't dig up flowers for many years.

Tips: A charming spring flower used not nearly enough.

Lily

Season: Blooms from June to September, depending on variety.

Description: Trumpets, chalices, etc., in a wide range of colors borne on handsome leafed stalks from one to six feet tall.

Uses: In borders, in beds, as specimens, and for cutting.

Culture: Plant fou. times the size of the bulb, spacing from six to 18 inches apart, depending on variety.

Light: Does well in full sun to partial shade, but shade produces a flower more true to color. Sun fades color.

Soil: Prefers deeply prepared, well-drained, fertile, neutral or slightly acidic soil.

Propagation: Multiplies readily and should be dug and replanted when crowded. Also can be grown from seed, scales, or bulblets.

Tips: One of the most rewarding of all flowers. New varieties are splendid, culture easy for most. Stay away from rarer varieties: many are quite fussy about conditions. However, many easily grown varieties are spectacular. Once planted, requires little care and lasts for years.

Muscari
(Also Called Grape Hyacinth)

Season: Blooms from March to June, depending on variety. The most popular varieties bloom early.

Description: Clear-blue giant flowers that resemble upside-down bunches of grapes. Green, grasslike foliage can look untidy at some periods of the year. Grows to six inches.

Uses: Good in rock gardens, naturalized, or bedded.

Culture: Plant in early fall, three inches deep and four inches apart.

Light: Grows in full sun or partial shade.

Soil: Prefers well-drained soil.

Propagation: Multiplies readily but will thrive for years without division. Divide to increase stock.

Tips: Armeniacum, Botryoides, Plumosum, Comosum, and Tubergenianum are blue in tone; *Botryoides album* is white. Can become a nuisance if allowed to run rampant. Keep under control and you will be rewarded with fine bloom.

Narcissus
(Also Called Daffodil and Jonquil)

Season: Blooms in April and May.

Description: Yellow, white, pink, apricot, and orange varieties. Leaves are green, slender, cylindrical, and rushlike. Some have large trumpets and others small ones. Endless number of varieties.

Uses: In borders, beds, or naturalized. Miniature are good in rock gardens. Good for cutting.

Culture: Plant in fall, six inches deep and six to nine inches apart.

Light: Likes sun or partial shade.

Soil: Almost any soil will do.

Propagation: Multiplies readily and rapidly. Dig every third or fourth year to increase stock. Or leave until flowers are not as prolific or large. This indicates overcrowding. Dig and replant.

Tips: Backbone of the spring garden. Try the newer varieties instead of sticking to the classic King Alfred or Mount Hood. Allow foliage to wither naturally before removing it. To keep it tidy, tie in bunches until it withers.

Ornithogalum
(Also Called Star of Bethlehem)

Season: Blooms in early spring.

Description: Star-shaped white flowers with green backing. Foliage comes up in fall, remains all winter, and then dies back after bloom.

Uses: Good in rock gardens or as harbinger of spring.

Culture: Plant in fall, three inches deep and two inches apart.

Empress of China is a spectacular hybrid hardy lily.

Select various kinds of tulips and you'll be able to enjoy their flowers from early until late spring.

Light: Grows in sun or light shade.

Soil: Any good soil will do.

Propagation: Multiplies readily. Lift and divide every three years to increase stock.

Tips: Rather charming little flower, rarely used in this country. Worth a try.

Puschkinia

Season: Blooms early in the spring.

Description: A four-inch scillalike plant that grows with a whitish flower with deep-blue lines down the center of the petals.

Uses: Good in rock gardens or as a harbinger of spring.

Culture: Plant in the fall, two inches deep and two to three inches apart.

Light: Likes sun.

Soil: Prefers well-drained soil.

Propagation: Multiplies some.

Tips: Can look runty if weather in early spring is severe.

Scilla Hispanica
(Also Called Scilla Campanulata, Spanish Bluebells, and Scottish Bluebells)

Season: Blooms in April.

Description: Grows about one foot to twenty inches high. Bell-like flowers similar to individual flowers on hyacinths appear on tall stalks. Leaves are grasslike. Colors are blue, pink, and white.

Uses: Good for planting under evergreens, in the woods, or among ground cover.

Culture: Plant in fall, five inches deep and about four inches apart.

Light: Does extremely well in dense shade.

Soil: Prefers well-drained soil.

Propagation: Multiplies astoundingly. Dig every other year to build up stock. One bulb may well produce fifty in two years.

Tips: Splendid for shady areas, and one of the few plants that thrives in dense shade.

Scilla Sibirica
(Also Called Blue Squill)

Season: Blooms in April.

Description: Intense blue flowers that grow from four to six inches high.

Uses: Good for naturalizing, in rock gardens or to contrast with daffodils.

Culture: Plant in fall, three inches deep and four inches apart.

Light: Likes full sun.

Soil: Prefers well-drained soil.

Propagation: Multiplies readily. Lift every three or four years and divide for more stock.

Tips: The blue is so intense you will want to plant them all over the place. A good bet and often overlooked by the novice gardener.

Sternbergia

Season: Blooms in autumn.

Description: Grows eight inches tall and has large, yellow crocuslike flowers. Leaves follow bloom.

Uses: Good in rock gardens.

Culture: Plant in August, four to six inches deep and six inches apart.

Light: Likes sun and shelter.

Soil: Prefers heavy soil but will do well in ordinary soil.

Propagation: Divide every few years.

Tips: Pleasant autumn flowers but only for special places. Should be in rock gardens or at the very front of borders; otherwise overshadowed by the showier flowers of the fall.

Trillium
(Also Called Wake-robin)

Season: Blooms in May.

Description: Lovely white or pink flowers about two inches across on handsome foliage. A native American wild flower but sold by some bulb houses.

Uses: Lovely in the rock garden or in a woodland area.

Culture: Plant immediately after blooming or in the early fall. Enrich soil with good compost or leaf mold.

Light: Likes light shade.

Soil: Prefers fairly moist, deep but not wet soil. An abundance of humus helps it reach perfection.

Propagation: Lift and divide every three or four years.

Tips: Foliage dies down after blooming, so be sure to mark carefully where you plant so that you don't dig it up by mistake. Beautiful, unusual, and worth growing.

Tulip
(Darwin, Cottage, Lily, Parrot, Double-early and Single-early varieties)

Season: Most varieties bloom in May, but some bloom in late April.

Description: Bowl-shaped flowers of every imaginable color. Grows to a height of two feet. Some grow to three feet.

Uses: For formal beds or in informal borders.

Culture: Plant in late October or early November. Earlier planting is a mistake. Place seven or eight inches deep in hole enriched with bone meal or Milorganite. Space six inches apart.

Light: Generally loves sun, but light shade will suffice.

Soil: Almost any soil that is not waterlogged will do.

Propagation: Buy new bulbs when yours run out.

Tips: Splendid. Every garden should have some. You may have luck and enjoy blooms for many years, but most conditions assure one good year of bloom, perhaps two. After two years, dig up and put in a cutting garden. Do not cut foliage until it has died down.

Tulip
(Kaufmania, Gregii, Fosteriana, and Other Botanical Tulips)

Season: Blooms from March through May.

Description: Small or large, low-growing, and should be investigated.

Uses: Good in rock gardens, in borders, or as contrast with early blooming bulbs.

Culture: Same as other tulips.

Light: Same as other tulips.

Soil: Same as other tulips.

Propagation: Same as other tulips.

Tips: Many very unusual varieties are available. Often these varieties last many years, in contrast to the usual type of tulip. Good drainage is essential, however. Not used nearly enough in this country.

Gladiola are the tender bulb flowers featured in this bouquet, along with cockscomb heads and dumb-cane leaves.

8
Tender Bulbs

Tender bulbs include all bulblike plants which grow from corms, rhizomes, tubers, and bulbs. Their variety is extensive, and they add a somewhat exotic effect to a garden. Their colors, shapes, and forms are fascinating, and many of them are rarely seen in the average garden. For a touch of class, use them freely. Many gardeners shy away from tender bulbs because they must be dug up in the fall and cured. But this rarely takes more than a few minutes, and the fine bloom is worth the inconvenience.

Digging them is the easiest way to assure their life; however, there are many borderline cases. Some are hardy in coastal areas, while a mere twenty or thirty miles inland they may die of the cold during the winter. They can be protected in some areas with mulches of hay, straw, dry leaves, or other materials, or they can be grown in cold frames. To be sure, dig them and store them indoors during the winter.

List of Tender Bulbs

The following list includes tender bulbs that are dormant in the winter and should be stored indoors.

Acidanthera

Season: Blooms from late July until late September.

Description: Highly fragrant flowers, white with purple throats. Two to three feet high.

Uses: Pleasant in borders and superb as cut flowers. One blossom scents an entire room.

Culture: Acidanthera is related to gladiolus, and the culture is similar. Plant corms outdoors early in the spring after soil has warmed. Place four inches deep and five inches apart.

Light: Likes full sun.

Soil: Prefers gritty, well-drained soil, enriched with leaf mold, compost, well-rotted manure, and some bone meal or Milorganite.

Propagation: See Gladiolus, page 73.

Winter Care: See Gladiolus, page 73.

Tips: Hardy in the South. Do not lift in autumn. Dig, divide, and reset every third or fourth spring before the growth begins. Beautifully fragrant. Not used nearly as much as it should be.

Caladium

Season: Has foliage all season.

Description: Heart-shaped leaves variegated with green, pink, red, and white in many patterns. Grows from one to two feet high.

Uses: Grown for foliage. Attractive in summer beds, in window boxes, and as indoor potted plants.

Culture: See Tuberous Begonia, page 75.

Light: Likes light shade.

Soil: Prefers rich, fairly loose, moist soil.

Winter Care: See Tuberous Begonia, page 75.

Tips: Excellent for shady areas of the garden.

Canna

Season: Blooms throughout the summer and fall.

Description: Spectacular flowers of cream, yellow, orange, pink, and red on large green- or bronze-leafed plants. Varieties grow from two and a half to five feet tall.

Uses: Good for beds, borders, boxes, or tubs.

Culture: Plant in spring after killing frosts. In the North, start tubers indoors four to eight weeks before outdoor planting time. Place in flats filled with peat moss. Keep damp. When tubers sprout, place in sunny window. Plant outdoors so that top of tuber is two inches below the soil surface.

Light: Likes full sun.

Soil: Prefers deep, fertile soil.

Winter Care: After killing frost, cut tops down and dig tubers with soil adhering to roots. Store in dry soil or sand at forty to fifty degrees.

Tips: Hardy in the South. Very flamboyant and should be used with restraint. Water frequently during hot summer months.

Colocasia
(Also Called Elephant's Ear)

Season: Has foliage all season.

Description: No flowers. Immense, heart-shaped, dark-green leaves from six to nine feet tall.

Uses: Grown for foliage. Especially attractive next to water. Good in beds, borders, and wooded glens.

Culture: Start tubers indoors some eight to ten weeks before soil warms up. Set out in May, three to six feet apart.

Light: Likes light shade.

Soil: Prefers rich, moist soil. Keep protected from wind.

Winter Care: Dig after killing frost. Store in dry soil or sand at forty to fifty degrees.

Tips: Hardy in deep south. Great conversation plant.

Dahlia

Season: Blooms from midsummer until killing frost.

Description: An almost limitless variety of shapes, sizes, and colors of flowers, borne on handsome bushy plants with dark-green foliage. Height varies from one to six feet.

Uses: Very versatile. Use for bedding, in borders, in window boxes, in tubs, and for cutting.

Culture: Plant tubers outdoors after danger of frost. It is safe to plant them when you plant

Dahlias are available in many sizes from one to six feet.

tomatoes. Set six inches deep and anywhere from one to three feet apart, depending on variety.

Light: Likes full sun but will tolerate light shade.

Soil: Ordinary, well-drained soil is suitable, but it should be enriched.

Propagation: Divide old tubers into separate tubers in spring. Be sure a small piece of the old stem is attached to each.

Winter Care: In fall, after killing frost, cut off the stems at a length of six inches and carefully lift tubers. Remove excess dirt, turn them upside down, and let them dry in a warm place. After they have dried, store in dry sand, peat moss, or vermiculite in a temperature of about forty-five degrees.

Tips: Easy to grow. Pinching out the tip of the young plant when its second or third pair of leaves has formed produces a finer specimen.

Galtonia
(Also Called Summer Hyacinth)

Season: Blooms from August to September.

Description: Bell-shaped, fragrant white flowers that grow to a height of from one and a half to three feet.

Uses: Nice for cutting or in beds.

Culture: Plant in spring after soil has warmed up. Place six inches deep and about one foot apart.

Light: Likes full sun.

Soil: Average soil will do.

Winter Care: Dig bulbs after killing frost. Store in a dark, dry, airy place at a temperature of from forty to fifty degrees.

Tips: Hardy where winters are not severe.

Gladiolus

Season: Blooms from July to September, depending on when planted.

Description: Spectacular, erect spikes of flowers on plants bearing swordlike leaves in all colors except blue. Grows from two to three feet tall.

Uses: Best for cutting but can be used effectively in borders or beds if restraint is practiced.

Culture: Plant corms after danger of frost. For succession of bloom, plant at two-week in-

White-and-green caladiums are beautiful in part shade.

tervals until ten weeks before first expected frost. Set corms four to five inches deep and four inches apart in rows eighteen inches apart for cut flowers or eight inches apart for beds and borders. Stake them to prevent wind damage. Water well during dry periods.

Light: Likes full sun.

Soil: Prefers well-drained average soil.

Propagation: Corms multiply readily. Tiny cormels, which are attached to the new season's corm, can be sown like seed in spring. They bloom in three years.

Winter Care: In the fall, allow foliage to die naturally. Before heavy frost, dig plants carefully. Cut foliage one-half inch above the new corms that have formed above the old corms. Air them in a cool frost-free place. When dry, clean and discard the old corms and roots. Store in a dry place at fifty degrees.

Tips: Pick when lowest flower is half open. Pinch off top bud.

At Antonellis in Santa Cruz, California, cascade tuberous begonias hang from lath; you can hang them from a tree.

Hymenocallis
(Also Called Ismenes, Spider Lily, Peruvian Daffodil, Basket Flowers)

Season: Blooms in June and July.

Description: Grows from fifteen to twenty-four inches high with medium-green foliage and highly fragrant pure-white flowers.

Uses: Particularly beautiful. Can be used as specimen plant in rock gardens or borders. Unusually fragrant. Good for cuttings.

Culture: Plant bulbs in the spring after soil has become thoroughly warm, four inches deep and eight to ten inches apart.

Light: Likes full sun or half shade.

Soil: Prefers well-drained soil that is deeply enriched with bone meal, blood meal or Milorganite.

Propagation: Bulbs multiply somewhat over the years.

Winter Care: In the fall, before heavy frost, dig the bulbs and bring them indoors. Spread them out in a dry place to ripen. When ripe, cut off the withered tops and store them over the winter in a cool, dry place.

Tips: Particularly hardy in the South. Do not dig up in the fall.

Polianthes
(Also Called Tuberose)

Season: Blooms during the summer.

Description: Highly fragrant white flowers on handsome foliage some two and a half to four feet in height.

Uses: Good for cutting or in beds and borders.

Culture: Plant after soil has warmed in the spring, three inches deep and six inches apart.

Light: Likes full sun.

Soil: Prefers rich, well-drained soil.

Winter Care: In the fall, dig before heavy frost. Cure, dry, and place in a bag of vermiculate, perlite, or dry sand. Store in a dry place, preferably at sixty to sixty-five degrees.

Tips: If the temperature during winter storage is too cool, may not bloom the following year. Best to buy new bulbs each spring. They are inexpensive enough to replace each year. Hardy in the South.

Tigridia
(Also Called Tiger Flower, Tiger Iris, Mexican Shellflower)

Season: Blooms in July and August.

Tuberous begonias will also grow well planted in the garden in soil that is moist and humusy in part shade.

Description: Large brilliantly colored, bowl-shaped flowers that bloom only one day, but a succession of bloom takes place throughout the blooming period. Colors are red, white, yellow, and combinations.

Uses: Colorful in borders and beds.

Culture: Plant corms outdoors in spring after weather is warm. Plant three inches deep and five to six inches apart. Mulch when shoots are three to four inches high.

Light: Likes full sun.

Soil: Prefers rich, well-drained soil.

Propagation: Corms multiply readily. Divide when ready to plant in the spring.

Winter Care: Dig before heavy frost in the fall. Tie in small bundles and hang in a cool, airy, frost-free place until spring.

Tips: Hardy in the South. Do not dig in fall. Some claim that they are hardy where temperatures do not fall below zero with regularity.

Tuberous Begonia

Season: Blooms all summer and into the fall.

Description: Flowers come in a wide range of colors and types. Some are upright, some hang-ing. Grows from one to three feet high.

Uses: Excellent for window boxes and pots.

Culture: Start indoors six to eight weeks before soil warms up. Place in peat moss, keep moist, and when it has sprouted, move into light. But do *not* place in direct sunlight. Plant outdoors, two to three inches deep and about one foot apart. Stake when one foot high. Hanging varieties are started the same way, but plant in hanging basket (three per large basket).

Light: Needs good light but *little* or *no* direct sunlight.

Soil: Prefers loose, fertile, well-drained soil that contains a lot of organic matter. Keep moist.

Propagation: Difficult, but with much experience can be successful. Not for beginners.

Winter Care: Before killing frost, dig entire plants with earth attached and place in warm, dry place. Clean tubers after the tops have completely died and store in temperature of fifty to fifty-five degrees. Can be difficult but inexpensive to replace.

Tips: Ideal for shady locations. Hanging types are sensational.

Trumpet vine, a thunbergia relative, is an all-time favorite for covering trellises, arbors and fences.

9
Climbing Flowering Plants

An area of flower gardening largely overlooked by most gardeners is the growth and culture of climbing flowering plants. These delightful specimens can be grown against any upright surface. Walls and fences, tree stumps, unsightly posts, and other objects provide ideal support for climbing plants. They take little garden space to grow, and at the same time, they can be used to provide shade and privacy or to fill in while foundation plantings grow.

If you wish to grow them on walls, you will have to install a trellis, or rig up a series of strings or wires for them to grow on. A plastic netting available at most garden centers is ideal for their culture. When you install the necessary support, be sure it stands from three to six inches away from the wall surface you are going to cover. This minimizes the danger of damage to plants from reflected heat and allows for thickening of the vines as they grow.

List of Climbing Flowering Plants

All but one of the plants listed below are annuals, so you don't have to worry about providing special trellises which can be removed to facilitate painting. One perennial, clematis, is included. This does not pose any special problems. Simply train the plant on the trellis against the wall, and when it is time to paint, lower the trellis to the ground along with the vines which have grown on it.

One other consideration to keep in mind is that, if you have planted your climbing plants on the side of a house, the eaves above may block off some of the rain. So be sure to water your plants regularly.

Canary Creeper
(Also Called Tropaeolum)

Season: Blooms from summer until fall.

Description: Graceful, dainty climber with beautifully cut foliage and finely fringed, rich canary-yellow, nasturtiumlike flowers. More unusual varieties bloom in the red range as well as white. Seven feet high.

Uses: Good for covering fences and other supports.

Culture: Sow in spring where plants are to flower and thin to six inches apart.

Light: Likes semishade.

Soil: Prefers fairly moist soil.

Cardinal Climber

Season: Blooms from summer until fall.

Description: White-throated, cardinal-scarlet blooms one to one and a half inches across contrast with glossy dark-green foliage.

Uses: Grown for display rather than shade.

Culture: Sow seed indoors in spring in the North about six weeks before soil warms up. In South, sow directly outdoors.

Light: Likes full sun or light shade.

Soil: Average soil will do.

Tips: Easy to grow and fast growing.

Clematis

Season: Blooms from spring to fall, depending on variety.

Description: A perennial vine. Colors range from reds and blues to whites and purples. Foliage is handsome, and blossoms are large.

Uses: On trellises, as screening, along fences, or on posts, arbors, or other garden structures.

Culture: Some care must be taken in growing clematis. First of all, soil should be alkaline, so each year put a handful of lime around the roots. Base should be in the shade, so plant a ground cover or flower to provide shade. This keeps the roots cool, which clematis needs. You can even place a slab, stone, or piece of slate on the ground over the roots. Dig a big hole, fortify it with fertilizer, add some lime, and plant.

Light: Likes shade on its roots, sun on its upper regions. Grows to find the sun.

Soil: Prefers rich, alkaline soil.

Tips: Buy from your nursery or from a reliable mail-order house.

Comtesse de Bouchard is a hybrid clematis.

Cup-and-Saucer Vine
(Also Called Cobaea and Cathedral Bells)

Season: Blooms from summer until fall.

Description: Attractive two and a quarter-inch bell-shaped blooms that are clear green until they fully open, when they turn a rich purple-blue. Then they bear large, plum-shaped fruits. Grows to twenty feet.

Uses: For shade and screening.

Culture: Sow seed indoors and transplant to garden when weather has warmed. Plant in the place where you want them to grow, since they resent being transplanted.

Light: Suitable for sun or partial shade.

Soil: Ordinary soil will do.

Tips: Resists to insects and disease well.

Morning Glory and Moonflower

Season: Blooms from midsummer until frost.

Description: Vines grow to eight feet and higher. Prolific bloom in blue, white, crimson, and violet shades.

Uses: For providing shade, and to grow on trellises on sides of buildings or garden structures.

Culture: Plant outdoors in spring after danger of frost has passed. To hasten germination, nick shell for each seed with a knife and soak for forty-eight hours in tepid water before planting. Plant them where you want them to grow, since they resent being transplanted.

Light: Likes full sun.

Soil: Ordinary soil will do.

Tips: Morning Glory blooms in the daytime and white moonflower blooms at night.

Thunbergia
(Also Called Black-eyed Susan Vine)

Season: Blooms from summer until fall.

Description: Pretty little climber with flowers ranging in color from yellow and orange to pure white. Grows to five feet high.

Uses: Especially useful for low trellises, hanging baskets, and even in flower beds.

Culture: Sow indoors six weeks before weather has warmed. Transplant to place where you wish it to grow.

Light: Likes full sun to light shade.

Soil: Ordinary soil will do.

Thunbergia is available with black-centered orange flowers; excellent for trellises and baskets.

White Wings thunbergia has snowy flowers.

Aubrietia makes a beautiful cascade of foliage and flowers when planted at the top of a rock outcropping.

10
Rock Gardens

Rock gardens are difficult, so before you install one, be sure you know what you are doing. A rock garden of the best kind absolutely depends on the outcropping of stones or boulders. If you have natural outcroppings of rock on your property, you are several steps ahead of the game, because you can plan around them. If you do not, plan carefully. That is not to say that the problems are insurmountable. Effective rock gardens have been constructed on perfectly flat surfaces.

Essentially, when you install a rock garden, you are re-creating the majesty of nature on a small scale. Therefore, avoid any feeling of artificiality. For example, lava rock may look perfectly fine on the slopes of Mount Vesuvius, but it has no place in Kansas City or Philadelphia. Use the rocks which are native to your locality, and you are well on your way to designing a successful rock garden. Visit well-designed rock gardens in your locality and learn from them. Walk around in areas where natural outcrops of rocks occur. Notice how the rocks jut out of the ground.

Designing a Rock Garden

Keep in mind that a well-cared-for garden requires a good deal of attention, so it is usually better to design a small rock garden rather than a large one. A small manicured garden looks infinitely better than a large unkempt one. Even if you plan on unusual features such as banks, pools, or waterfalls, it is better to keep your garden small.

Since you are in a sense re-creating nature, proportion is very important. Do not use rocks that are too small and do not use rocks that are all roughly the same size. Nature doesn't work that way, and your garden shouldn't either. Here and there in your garden, place several medium-sized stones together to give an illusion of a more massive outcropping. Remember contrast. The gentle slopes and flat areas with little or no rock showing are just as important as the massive outcroppings. These flat rockless areas should be placed between the bolder, rocky outcroppings. Nothing could be more boring than a rock garden with evenly placed, similar-sized rocks.

Selection of Rocks and Preparation of Soil

As mentioned above, select rocks that blend in with the immediate surroundings. Sandstone and water-worn limestone are recommended because they are reasonably soft and retain some moisture. However, almost any kind of rock will suffice. When you plan your garden, try to use the same kind of stone throughout. This gives a feeling of unity in your scheme. You will want several very large rocks.

When you prepare the soil, be sure that it is reasonably fertile and porous and that the drainage is good. If you are saddled with heavy soil, break up the subsoil thoroughly, working in a good deal of sand, coal cinders, or broken brick. Add a good amount of compost, peat moss, or other decayed organic matter. Throughout the garden the soil should be at least eight to twelve inches deep. Some rock garden plants will grow in shallow soil, but most prefer a deeper soil. You might want to plant one area with acid-loving plants and another with alkaline-loving plants. Modify these portions of your garden accordingly with acidic peat moss or lime. Mix in some bone meal, and your soil is set.

How to Build a Rock Garden from Scratch

Step one in the construction of a rock garden is to grade the soil. If you are blessed with a naturally sloping surface, a few changes may be all that's needed; but if your land is flat, you will have to build up the hills and dales, modify slopes, and provide for a path. You can dig out the lows and use this soil to provide the highs. Once you have graded your garden, it is time to place the rocks. Start at the lowest part of the garden and work up. Keep in mind that in nature, about two-thirds of most rocks are buried in the soil. Also remember that stones have strata or layer markings on them. Try to keep these uniform among the rocks you use. And for the best effect, keep the strata running at a slight angle to the horizontal. Also, reveal the weathered faces of the rocks.

Dwarf hardy asters give fall bloom in a rock garden.

When you place your rocks, be sure to set them firmly in the soil. Buttress them with soil and small stones, and tilt them slightly backward into the bank so that rain will drain into the soil and keep your plants well watered. After you have placed each stone, step back, look over your work, and make revisions. It's important that the larger rocks look as though what you see is merely a small outcropping of what lies below.

Plan your path through your garden. Allow it to twist and turn as it would under natural circumstances. Finally, don't abruptly end your rock garden. Let it trail off gradually, with a rock here and a rock there. In this way, it will appear to be more natural.

Selecting the Plants for Your Garden

Make things easy for yourself. Choose only hardy plants that can remain in your rock garden permanently. Look around at other rock gardens in your area, ask questions, find out what will grow, check with your local nursery, and then proceed to purchase your plants. Whatever you do, don't be tempted by plants that grow so vigorously that they may take over the garden and drive everything else out.

Ideally, you should have plants that are permanent, are hardy, and can be kept under control with little effort.

At the same time, part of the challenge of gardening is attempting to grow something that takes just a little bit of skill. Reserve a few spots in your rock garden for such experimentation. If you succeed with a difficult plant, your ego will receive a boost, and you will have something just a little bit different from that of your friends and neighbors. You will have to study the idiosyncrasies of the rarer forms and accommodate them in your scheme. And if you get hooked on rock gardening, you will undoubtedly study the form, experiment, and probably come up with a garden that is quite special.

When to Plant Your Garden

You can plant a rock garden in either the spring or early fall. Fall is more advantageous than spring, because you will not have to water your garden as frequently. If you plant during the summer with stock bought at a nursery, be sure to water regularly and perhaps provide shade from the hot summer sun. Your nursery can advise you about this.

How to Arrange Your Plants

Again, try to imitate nature. A planting of allium bulbs could follow a long crevice. Some pinks can be placed so that they appear to be cascading down a cliff. Then, plant some smaller plants of the same variety at the base of the cliff, making them appear as if they had grown by chance from seeds dropped from the larger plant. The flat areas should have creeping plants growing on them. Bulbs should be placed informally here and there. Don't confine yourself to the spring blooming bulbs. Include some that bloom in summer and the autumn crocus as well.

Plant your specimens in groups for the most part. Here and there a single plant of a single variety may be placed, but if you use all single specimens the effect will be spotty and unnatural. Keep in mind that there are some beautiful dwarf trees (both deciduous and evergreen), as well as shrubs, which can be quite effective in rock gardens.

Try to give your garden a backdrop. Flowering evergreens are a good bet if they are planted informally. Whatever you do, don't place a formal hedge behind your garden. The entire effect of duplicating nature would be defeated by the stiffness of the background.

Mulching Your Garden

After you have planted your garden, mulch it. Use crushed stone in parts of the garden. This carries out your rock-strewn effect. Don't use stones of uniform size. This is not how nature works. Be sure the stones vary from the size of a pea to the size of a walnut with a few larger. In shaded parts of the garden, use a mulch of compost or peat moss. In the woods, the ground is covered with organic matter, so the mulch will simulate natural conditions.

Caring for Your Garden Through the Winter

In colder sections of the country, you should cover your rock garden with evergreen branches or salt hay *after* the ground has frozen to a depth of one or two inches. This usually takes place in late December or January. The purpose of a winter ground cover is not to keep the ground warm but to keep it frozen. It is the alternate freezing and thawing of the ground that creates winterkill in the plant world. Old Christmas trees make ideal ground cover. Do not use leaves. They mat down and suffocate plants.

Maintenance Through the Years

Since you have constructed a garden with highs and lows, slopes and cliffs, there is always the danger of soil erosion. One driving rain storm could wash away a substantial amount of the soil in your garden. A top dressing of soil once a year is called for. Mix it with some bone meal and spread about one-half to one inch of this mixture among, between, and under the plants. One last precaution: rock gardens are particularly vulnerable to slugs. Watch for them. If you see any, get busy with an effective slug killer.

Lists of Suitable Rock Garden Plants

Perennials

Research the following in Chapter 4. Dwarf varieties are available.

  Achillea, or yarrow
  Ajuga, or bugleweed
  Alyssum, or basket of gold
  Anemone, or windflower
  Arabis, or rock cress
  Aster
  Astilbe, or spirea
  Bleeding heart, or dicentra (dwarf is called Dutchman's breeches)
  Candytuft, or iberis
  Columbine, or aquilegia
  Dianthus, or garden pink
  Flax, or linum
  Iris
  Phlox
  Primrose, or primula
  Veronica, or speedwell

Enjoy achillea flowers outdoors, or cut for bouquets.

Hardy Bulbs

The following bulbs are appropriate for rock gardens. Read about them in Chapter 7.

Allium	Leucojum
Camassia	Lily
Chionodoxa	Muscari
Crocus	Narcissus
Eranthis	Puschkinia
Fritillaria	Scilla
Galanthus	Tulip

Other Rock Garden Plants

The following plants, all suitable for rock gardens, are sometimes difficult to purchase, since they are not generally stocked by most nurseries. Most will thrive in sun and well-drained soil.

Sedum spectabile is extremely easy to grow; fall flowers.

Hardy sedums and sempervivums can be spectacular, as these are, when planted in a sunny rock wall garden.

Aethionema, or Warley Rose: Six inches high. Shrublike with masses of rich rose-red flowers in summer.

Androsace, or Rock Jasmine: Five-inch-high mats of gray-leaved rosettes with round heads of deep-pink flowers. Blooms in spring. May need winter protection.

Antennaria, or Pussytoes: Three to six inches high. Gray-leaved carpet-type plant with tiny, tasseled flowers in white or pink.

Arenaria, or Sandwort: Six-inch-high needlelike leaves with large, white flowers.

Armeria, or Thrift: Six- to eight-inch-high cushions studded with stemless rose-red flowers from spring on.

Artemesia, or Wormwood: Four to eight inches high. Grown for foliage. When flower spikes develop, cut them off.

Aubrietia: Purplish or pink flowers.

Calamintha: Four-inch-high mats on plant with tiny white and purple flowers.

Ceratostigma, or Plumbago: Six to ten inches high. Spreading mat-forming plant with green or bronze leaves and deep-blue flowers. Blooms in late summer and fall.

Chrysogonum, or Golden Start: Four to eight inches high. Slow spreading clumps of hairy foliage and bright-yellow flowers about one inch in diameter. Blooms for a long while in the summer. Prefers partial shade.

Cornus: Six to eight inches high. A low ground cover with white flowers resembling flowering dogwood. Red berries appear in the fall. Needs moist, acidic soil and shade.

Corydalis: Six to eight inches high. Tuberous flowers in deep rose, purple, and yellow.

Cotoneaster: Several varieties are dwarf. They grow flat, are evergreen, and bear red berries. Flowers are white or pink.

Cymbalaria: Low, trailing plants with small leaves and flowers resembling snapdragons. Needs moist soil and shade. Lilac-blue or lavender flower with yellow throat.

Daphne: Low shrub with clusters of pink flowers in spring. Should have well-drained, peaty soil. White-flowered varieties have variegated leaves.

Douglasia: Prostrate plants with tiny leaves and scented yellow flowers in the spring. For light shade and limy soil.

Draba: Two to four inches high. Cushion plants with yellow flowers. Needs gritty soil and full sun.

Dryas: Creeping shrub with small, oaklike, dark-green leaves and large, yellow-eyed, white flowers. Blooms in summer.

Edrianthus: Lovely silver-gray cushion with pale-blue bells blooming in spring. Needs sun and gritty soil.

Epigaea, or Trailing Arbutus: Difficult to grow but rewarding if you can do it. Fragrant pink or white flowers on three-inch stems in spring. Needs acidic, sandy, peaty soil and shade.

Epimedium, or Barrenwort: Nine to twelve inches high. Good for semishade or woodland conditions. White, yellow, and red flowers on wiry stems.

Erica, or Heath: Dwarf shrubs to one foot high. Red flowers in spring. Prefers sandy, peaty, acidic soil.

Erigeron, or Fleabane: Six-inch-high tufted plant with white or pink daisies. Blooms from spring until fall. Prefers poor, sandy soil.

Erinus: Two- to four-inch flowers in rosy purple or white. Good for crevices. Prefers shade. Where winters are very cold, it does not survive but often reseeds itself.

Erodium: One- to three-inch-high gray-green mat. Ferny foliage with white to deep-pink flowers. Blooms through summer into autumn.

Festuca, or Fescue: Six- to nine-inch-high ornamental grass with blue leaves and creamy flowers.

Genista, or Broom: Dwarf shrubs from one to two feet high. Flowers are golden yellow. Blooms in early summer and likes well-drained soil.

Gentiana, or Gentian: Two to four inches high. Big blue trumpets in the spring and again in the summer. Prefers good loam. Many are difficult to grow.

Geranium: Some varieties are suitable. Red flowers through summer.

Globularia: Prostrate-growing evergreens. Blue balls of flowers appear on short stems in summer. Likes full sun.

Houstonia, or Bluet: Low-growing plant that blooms in spring and early summer. Prefer moist soil and shade. Flowers are deep blue.

Hutchinsia: Low, rounded cushions with pure-white flowers in the spring. Likes a cool spot with partial shade.

Hypericum, or St. John's Wort: Six to nine inches high. Likes sun. Bright-yellow flowers.

Lewisia: Grows up to eight inches high. Blooms in spring and early summer. Flowers are pink and white. Likes gritty soil.

Lithospermum: Thick mats of gentian-blue flowers throughout summer. Prostrate. Needs neutral or acidic soil.

Lysimachia: Vigorous prostrate spreader with yellow flowers in summer. Tends to become a nuisance.

Mazus: White- and yellow-centered lavender-blue flowers. Grows one inch high. Grows in moist soil. Needs light shade.

Mentha: Carpets of peppermint-scented leaves with tiny lilac flowers. Needs moist soil and shade.

Mitchella, or Partridgeberry: Small evergreen trailer with white flowers followed by red berries. Needs shade and woodland soil.

Omphalodes, or Navelwort: Six- to eight-inch-high plants with blue flowers in summer. Prefers shade.

Opuntia: Hardy cactus, low and spreading. Two-inch yellow flowers in summer. Full sun.

Oxalis: Not hardy where winters are severe. Four- to six-inch gray leaves with funnel-shaped flowers of gold and pink.

Succulents and rocks make natural garden companions.

Penstemon, or Beard Tongue: Shrubby plants with blue, purple, and lavender flowers. Not too hardy.

Polemonium: Ten- to fifteen-inch-high plants with pink or blue flowers. Easy to grow, blooms in spring on fernlike plants. Needs rich, moist soil and some shade.

Potentilla: Low-growing (one- to eight-inch-high) plants. Colors are white, yellow, crimson, and apricot. Foliage is silvery. Different varieties bloom from spring through summer.

Pyrola, or Shinleaf: Eight-inch-high plants with white flowers. Requires shade and woody soil.

Rhodohypoxis: Four-inch-high plants with red flowers. Likes sun and moist soil. Blooms through summer but is best where summer is cool and winter mild.

Saponaria, or Soapwort: Trailing plant with bright-pink flowers in summer. Can become a nuisance.

Saxifraga: Many varieties in many colors. Grows around six inches high. Silvery leaves with white, yellow, or red flowers. Likes gritty soil on the alkaline side.

Sedum: Dozens of varieties, low growing with flowers of many colors.

Sempervivum, or Houseleek: Sun-loving plants, rosettes of fleshy leaves in green, purples, or reds. Flowers are star-shaped in white cream, pink, or red.

Silene, or Catchfly: Six- to eight-inch-high plants. Tufted green foliage with white or pink flowers. Blooms from June to August.

Sisyrinchium: Easy-to-grow bright-yellow flowers on six- to nine-inch-high plants. Blooms in midsummer.

Teucrium: Low-growing shrubs about one foot high with reddish-purple flowers in summer.

Thalictrum: Need semishade and moist woodland soil. Flowers are purple on three-inch variety and yellow on twelve-inch variety.

Thymus, or Thyme: Showy and easy to grow, one- to three-inch mats with purple flowers. Some varieties have white, pink, or crimson flowers. Does well in dry, hot conditions.

Tunica: Six- to nine-inch-high plants with small, pink flowers.

Your best ally against diseases and pests is to know the needs of each plant—and provide them.
Impatiens like these growing in larger pottery containers, for example, need mostly shade and
soil that is always evenly moist.

11
Plant Diseases and Pests

Just as animals suffer from various diseases, so flowers are subject to pests and diseases, which can injure or even kill them. All types of plants—annuals, perennials, biennials, hardy and tender bulbs, and climbing plants—can be the objects of parasites, fungi, and insects. The best way to assure a flourishing, healthy garden is to be aware of the pests and diseases that may attack your plants. If you spot potential difficulties when they are just beginning, you can take the appropriate steps to protect your plants and to combat the predators.

Year in and year out new varieties of flowers are being developed by the breeders. Some of these new varieties are particularly disease or pest resistant. Plant these if you have the choice. On the other hand, many of the new varieties are not necessarily disease resistant. Be especially watchful of these new varieties.

If you grow one particular type of plant in the same place year in and year out you are asking for trouble. Many diseases live on a particular host plant during the summer and usually will persist somehow or other through the winter. When you plant the same variety in that spot, the parasite merely attacks the new growth and becomes an even greater menace. For this reason, it is wise rotate your crops; that is, plant gladiolus in one spot one year, and the following year, put them elsewhere. Plant marigolds in one spot one year, and the following year, change their location. If you don't do this, you might find that you have to fumigate the entire plot in order to grow anything in your soil.

How to Control Disease

There are many different methods of controlling plant diseases, but the best protection is to be aware of the needs of your flowers and to practice good cultivation so that the plants have a healthy, vigorous growth. Robust plants are more resistant to disease. Weak plants are more susceptible to attack by parasitic fungi, viruses, and pests.

Factors that favor the spread of disease include: purchasing poor-quality seed (from which only weak seedlings will grow); growing plants too close together; acidic soil; poor light; overfeeding with chemical fertilizers; and high temperatures. As far as disease is concerned, spraying, dusting, and fumigating are second in importance to good culture.

Follow instructions in preparing the soil and maintaining your plants. Provide proper drainage, air circulation, and sunshine. Keep in mind that some judicious pruning here and there during the season is a great aid.

Weeds are not only unsightly but they also act as alternate host plants to many fungous diseases, which thrive on them and then infect cultivated plants. A weed like shepherd's purse may carry clubroot, which will infect wallflowers. Plantains often carry the virus of spotted wilt. Ground cherry may harbor mosaic virus. Keep your garden weeded.

Hygiene is also important. When you find some infected foliage, remove and burn it. Do not let decaying plant material sit around near the garden. Remove and burn dead or dying branches from nearby trees or bushes. Above all, do not put any infected material on your compost heap. That is just asking for future trouble.

Space your plants so that there is plenty of air circulating among them. Dampness and poor circulation are responsible for many problems, so give your plants room.

D X Fenten* suggests the following list of rules when using chemical sprays.

1. Buy only what you need, and use what you buy. Don't buy one of each so you can be prepared for any eventuality while impressing your neighbors with your collection. Use your sprays and dusts in a regular program of preventive spraying. A thorough, effective protection program can eliminate a large percentage of garden problems.

2. If you have not sprayed preventively, or for one reason or another pests and diseases are attacking your plants, try to identify the problem and then treat it. General purpose mixtures are available and can be used successfully to control many insects and diseases of plants. However, in most cases, specific chemicals formulated for specific problems do a better, less expensive job.

3. Keep all garden chemicals out of the reach of children and pets. The best place for these chemicals is in a locked cabi-

net or closet. If locking them up is impossible, place them on a very high shelf.

4. Use only clean spray equipment. Clean out sprayers after each use by washing thoroughly in detergent and rinsing in clear water several times. Never leave chemicals in the spray equipment until "next time." This would ruin your spray equipment, and it would dilute the power of the chemical as well.

5. Spray carefully so that you cover all parts of the plant: the top and bottom of leaves, soil around the trunk, and the trunk itself. Cover thoroughly but do not soak. No dripping means poor coverage; too much dripping means wasted chemicals.

6. Never use the same sprayer for poisons (herbicides) as you use for other sprays, no matter how thoroughly you wash it between use. Even the slightest residue left by the herbicide can cause considerable damage to the plants. Keep two separate sprayers and label them clearly.

Spraying and Dusting Equipment

There are many different types of sprayers and dusters on the market. Pick one to suit your needs. The best type for most gardens is the compressed air sprayer. Generally, a single loading takes care of all of your spraying needs. Each tankful holds about one and a half gallons of spray, enough for the average garden. Compressed air sprayers retail for between ten and fifteen dollars.

Hose-end sprayers are limited in that they can only reach as far as the hose can reach. The trombone sprayer uses a pail for its supply of chemical solution. Consult your local nursery or plant store about your specific needs.

Pests That Attack Roses

Aphids
Aphids are pink or green minuscule insects

*Clear & Simple Gardening, Grosset & Dunlap, 1975.

that often cover the buds and stems of the rose. They suck out plant juices; stunt and deform the buds. They secrete a sticky substance that collects on the leaves.

Control: Spray with an all-purpose rose spray or dust.

Japanese Beetles

These are metallic green with coppery wing covers and are about a half inch long. They are a common pest in the eastern part of the United States. If you have them, you can't miss them. They eat flowers and leaves, often completely stripping your rose of its foliage.

Control: Spray infected bushes with carbaryl or an all-purpose spray as soon as beetles appear. Repeat the treatment every five to seven days as needed. Hand picking them is a cinch: fill a glass jar with chlorine or ammonia and push them off the plant into the jar. You will save yourself much trouble in subsequent years if you do this right away, since these beetles lay their eggs in the ground surrounding the infected plant.

Rose Chafer

Rose chafers are gray, long-legged beetles about one-half inch long that eat flowers and leaves. They can completely defoliate your rose bush.

Control: Use all-purpose rose spray or Methoxychlor.

Rose Curculio

This is a red-snouted beetle with black legs about one-quarter inch long. It eats holes in buds and leaves. Buds never open.

Control: Use all-purpose rose spray, dust, or Sevin.

Rose Leafhopper

This bug sucks juices from the underside of the leaves, which fade, turn yellow and then brown, and finally die. It is greenish in color, wedge-shaped, and about one-eighth inch long.

Control: Use all-purpose rose spray, dust, Pyrethrum, Methoxychlor, or Rotenone.

Rose Midge

Rose midges are tiny yellow-brown insects that eat buds, which turn black and never bloom.

Control: Use all-purpose rose spray or Sevin.

Rose Scale

These are white, round scaly insects about one-eighth inch across that suck plant juices. The plant is weakened and may die.

Control: Remove and burn all infested areas. Apply a dormant oil spray in the spring and later on use all-purpose rose spray or Malathion.

Rose Slug

There are many varieties of this insect. Most are yellowish green measuring from one-half to one inch in length. They will eat large holes in the leaves.

Control: Use all-purpose rose spray, Malathion, or arsenate of lead.

Rose-stem Girdler

These are small, white caterpillars that tunnel into stems, causing them to swell.

Control: Cut off and burn all infected shoots.

Spider Mite

Spider mites are almost-invisible, tiny, oval insects that feed on the underside of leaves, which become gray, red, or brown. The entire plant can be defoliated.

Control: Use all-purpose rose spray, Malathion, or Kelthane.

Thrip

This is a tiny, yellow-orange bug that feeds only on flowers. The buds turn brown and fail to open.

Control: Cut off diseased buds. Use all-purpose rose spray or Malathion.

Diseases That Affect Roses

Anthracnose

This fungus thrives in cool, wet weather. Dark spots with light centers appear on the leaves and canes.

Control: Rake up all leaves and burn them. Then spray with Captan, Fermate, or an all-purpose rose spray.

Black Spot

This is another fungus that thrives in cool, wet weather. Black spots appear on the leaves, which turn yellow and fall.

Control: Rake up all leaves and burn them. Then spray with Captan, Fermate, or an all-purpose rose spray.

Brown Canker

This fungus causes white spots with purple outside rings to appear on canes and leaves. It can kill the plant.

Control: Remove all diseased canes, use a Bordeaux mixture, and remove mulching from around the plant.

Leaf Spot

This fungus is carried on seeds, which remain in the soil. Brown spots with gray centers first appear on the leaves, which then turn brown and fall.

Control: Remove and burn all diseased leaves. Spray with Maneb or Zineb.

Mildew

This is another fungus that thrives in cool, wet weather. White powdery areas turn black, leaves are dwarfed, and buds are disfigured.

Control: Use Karathane or Piprin as soon as you notice the mildew. Follow up with Captan later.

Rust

This fungus also thrives in cool, wet weather. Orange spots appear on the leaves and canes, which eventually die.

Control: Remove and burn all infected leaves. Then use a Zineb or Bordeaux mixture.

Stem Canker

This fungus causes purple stripes to appear on the branches, which turn brown as the disease girdles the plant.

Control: Cut off the entire area to a point below the infection. Spray with Captan.

Pests That Attack Flowers

Ants

Some ants are lethal to certain varieties of plants. The black ant can do a great deal of damage. Ants nest under the ground, so borders and rock gardens are especially vulnerable to ant damage. The ants burrow and loosen the soil around the roots of your flowers, eventually causing them to wilt and die. If you see small piles of loose soil here and there, you have an ant problem. It's true that they feed on aphids, another pest, but the root damage they do necessitates ridding your garden of them.

Control: Inject Chlordane or Malathion into the holes with an oil gun.

Aphids

Aphids are the most abundant pests in the flower garden. They are tiny, green, lice-type bugs with wings. Keep a close watch for them, and even if you see just a few, destroy them immediately, since they multiply with frightening rapidity. They suck the juice from your plants, causing the buds and leaves to become disfigured. Many species also transmit virus diseases, which can reduce a crop or wipe it out together.

Control: Spray or dust with Malathion, rotenone, or nicotine sulfate. Repeat the application as necessary.

Asiatic Garden Beetles

This beetle is a reddish-brown creature that eats the leaves of plants during the night. In the daytime, it burrows under the soil near the base of the plant on which it is feeding. The larva form is a white grub that feeds on grass roots. It particularly likes the China Aster.

Control: Spray four level teaspoons of arsenate of lead in a gallon of water on the plants. Kill grubs by spraying the ground with chlordane or Dieldrin.

Blister Beetles

These gray-striped three-quarter-inch beetles eat the leaves of asters, calendula, marigold, phlox, and zinnia, as well as some other plants.

Control: Use Methoxychlor.

Cutworms

These are fat, green or brown caterpillars that gnaw away at the stems and leaves of your plants just at ground level. During the day, they hide under the surface of the vegetation. Eventually, they cause the plants to wilt and collapse. They are particularly fond of asters, carnations, chrysanthemums, dahlias, marigolds, rock garden plants and zinnias.

Control: Consult your nursery for cutworm bait. If the problem continues, the following year place tin cans with both ends removed around the plants when you put them in the ground.

Earwigs

European earwigs are about a half inch long and have a long, thin body. They eat both leaves and flowers of plants during the night. Chrysanthemums and dahlias are particularly susceptible.

Control: Keep the garden clear of piles of rubbish and rotting vegetation, which may provide shelter. Apply chlordane or lindane dust along fences or house foundations or spray the ground and lower parts of susceptible plants with carbaryl.

Japanese Beetles

These are metallic green with coppery wing covers and are about a half inch long. They are a common pest in the eastern part of the United States and feed on many plants. If you have them, you can't miss them. They eat flowers and leaves.

Control: Spray infected plants with carbaryl as soon as beetles appear. Repeat the treatment every five to seven days as needed. To hand pick them, fill a glass jar with chlorine or ammonia and push them into the jar.

Leafhoppers

Six-spotted leafhoppers cause leaves to curl and turn yellow. They are green, wedge-shaped, and about one-eighth inch long. They are a particularly serious problem because they can carry a virus, which can also infect your plants. They are fond of china asters, calendula, dahlia, gladiolus, marigold and zinnia.

Control: Use Sevin or Malathion.

Leaf Miners

Leaf miners are the larvae of flies and small moths, which feed on the internal tissues of leaves between the upper and lower surfaces. The pest subdivides into two categories. First there is the linear mine, which is a winding tunnel that grows wider as the larva grows, and then there is the blotch mine, which is a blisterlike cavity eaten out by one or more larvae. At first the damage is whitish, but it turns brown as the injured leaf tissue withers. Many garden plants are attacked by leaf miners, including asters, columbines, gladiolus and snapdragons. Sometimes chrysanthemums are attacked too.

Control: Destroy infected parts of plants and spray with Malathion as soon as the tunnels appear. Repeat the spray in two weeks.

Spider Mites

Spider mites are reddish in color and very small. They can do a lot of damage in a short span of time. They attack almost all plants, feeding on the underside of the leaves, where they lay round, reddish eggs. The leaves become finely speckled with yellow marks that spread until the leaves turn completely yellow and wither. When plants are heavily infested, the mites spin a fine webbing over the leaves. This is your signal to take steps to rid your plants of them.

Control: Use Malathion or Kelthane.

Stalk Borer

This brown caterpillar has brown or purple stripes and is about one inch long. It bores into stalks and can kill plants. It makes small holes in the stalks and leaves small droppings around the holes. Asters, columbines, cosmos, dahlias, delphiniums, irises, hollyhocks, and zinnias are affected.

Control: Keep the garden weed-free and use Sevin.

Tarnished Plant Bug

This is a small brownish bug that injects a toxin into the plant, causing shoots to blacken or flowers to be deformed. It is particularly fond of chrysanthemums and dahlias.

Control: Spray all susceptible plants with

carbaryl when the bugs first appear. Repeat at seven- to ten-day intervals to maintain control.

Thrip

Two types of thrips damage flowering plants. The gladiolus thrip is found on gladiolus and may even attack delphiniums, hollyhocks, freesias, ageratum, alyssum, asters, dahlias, dianthus, and marigolds.

The onion thrip attacks roses, peonies, and other plants. These tiny insects suck the sap of the leaves and flower petals, leaving white or yellow spots on the areas they have attacked. If allowed to flourish, misshapen flowers will result and often total wilting of the blooms before they have a chance to blossom.

Control: Spray with nicotine sulfate and soap or with phrethrum-rotenone insecticide. Cut off all diseased greenery.

Diseases That Affect Flowers

Blight

This fungus thrives in high humidity and poor air circulation. Chrysanthemums, dahlias, gladiolus, peonies, and snapdragons are most susceptible. Foliage, flowers, and stems suddenly spot and wilt.

Control: Use Captan or Zineb.

Bulb Rot

This bacteria affects many flowers grown from bulbs. The corms, tubers, or bulbs rot and may smell badly.

Control: Destroy affected bulbs or corms. Tubers and rhizomes can sometimes be saved by treating with Captan, Ferbam, or Zineb.

Leaf Spot

This fungus is carried on seeds and remains in the soil. Brown spots with gray centers appear on the leaves, which turn brown and fall.

Control: Remove and burn all infected areas. Then use Maned or Zineb.

Nematode

These tiny, wormlike parasites are found in most soils. Almost any plant can be affected. Plants will yellow, lose their vigor, and wilt in hot weather.

Control: Plant nematode-resistant varieties. Check with your county agent or your local nursery for recommended control.

Powdery Mildew

This fungus thrives in cool, wet weather and in shaded areas. Patches of white powder appear on the leaves. Plants are dwarfed and disfigured. Alyssum, calendulas, chrysanthemums, cosmos, dahlias, daisies, delphiniums, phlox, poppies, snapdragons, sweet peas and zinnias are all affected.

Control: Spray with Karathane or wetable sulfur regularly.

Rust

This fungus thrives in cool, wet weather. Orange spots appear on the leaves. The plant dies eventually unless the disease is controlled. Alyssum, asters, chrysanthemums, dianthus, hollyhocks, and snapdragons are affected.

Control: Plant rust-resistant varieties, particularly of snapdragons, which are highly susceptible to this disease. Remove and burn infected leaves. Then use Zineb or Bordeaux mixture.

Virus

Many virus diseases affect plants, and almost all plants are susceptible to them. The foliage becomes yellow and mottled. Plant parts become distorted.

Control: Plant virus-resistant varieties. Keep the planting area clean and weed-free. Burn all diseased plants.

Wilt

This fungus lives in the soil and enters the plant through the roots. The leaves yellow and the plants are stunted. The leaves begin to drop on one side and then on the other. Alyssum, asters, chrysanthemums, columbines, dahlias, dianthus, marigolds, peonies, and snapdragons can be affected.

Control: Grow wilt-resistant varieties. If situation persists, fumigate the soil. Spraying does not help.

Appendix

Best Flowers for Cutting

Achillea
Aster
Bells of Ireland
Calendula
Carnation
Celosia
Chrysanthemum
Columbine
Corepsis
Cornflower
Cosmos
Dahlia
Delphinium
Foxglove
Gaillardia
Gerbera
Gladiola
Gloriosa daisy
Gypsophila
Iris
Larkspur
Marigold
Peony
Petunia
Poppy
Pyrethrum
Rose
Scabiosa
Shasta daisy
Snapdragon
Stock
Sweet pea
Sweet sultan
Sweet william
Zinnia

Lavender
Lilac
Lily
Lily-of-the-valley
Mignonette
Mock orange
Nicotiana
Peony
Rose
Stock
Sweet pea
Tuberose
Wallflower
Wisteria

Flowers for Fragrance

Alyssum
Carnation
Heliotrope

Tall Flowers for Backgrounds

Canna
Celosia, tall
Cleome
Cosmos
Dahlia, tall
Delphinium
Foxglove
Gladiola
Hibiscus
Hollyhock
Marigold, tall
Nicotiana
Snapdragon, tall
Sunflower
Tithonia
Zinnia, tall

Plants for Partial Shade

Ageratum
Astilbe
Azalea
Begonia
Bleeding heart

Boston ivy
Caladium
Coleus
Coral bells
Ferns
Forget-me-not
Impatiens
Lily-of-the-valley
Mock orange
Nicotiana
Pachysandra
Pansy
Plumbago
Polyanthus
Sweet violet
Torenia
Vinca
Viola

Annuals for Cutting

Ageratum
Amaranthus
Baby's breath
Calendula
Clarkia
Chrysanthemum
Coreopsis
Cosmos
Gaillardia
Larkspur
Lupine
Marigold
Nasturtium
Pansy
Phlox
Pinks
Poppy
Scabiosa
Snapdragon
Stock

Plants for Window Boxes

Alyssum
Asparagus sprengeri
Begonia
Celosia, dwarf
Coleus

Geranium
Ivy
Lobelia
Marigold, dwarf
Petunia
Verbena
Vinca

Plants for Dry or Poor Soils

Alyssum
Bridal wreath
Cactus
California poppy
Candytuft
Celosia
Cleome
Coreopsis
Cosmos
Dianthus
Euphorbia
Four o'clock
Gaillardia
Gloriosa daisy
Gypsophila
Helianthemum
Honeysuckle
Iris
Linum
Lychnis
Marigold
Mugho pine
Nasturtium
Petunia
Phlox
Poppy
Portulaca
Potentilla (Gold Drop)
Verbena

Annuals for Very Dry Areas

Coreopsis
Four o'clock
Larkspur
Morning Glory
Phlox
Portulaca
Sunflower
Zinnia

Index